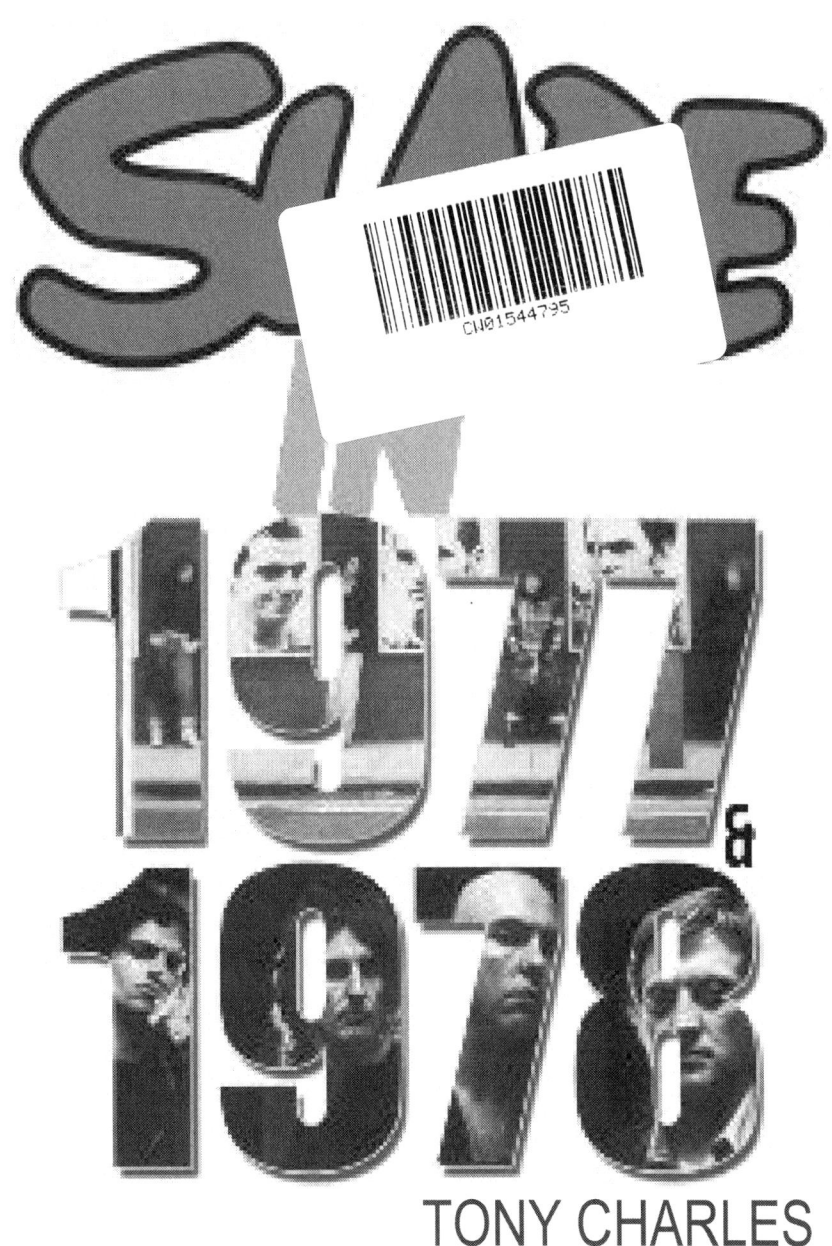

TONY CHARLES
POUK HILL PRESS

IN:FO
International

▶▶▶▶▶▶▶▶▶▶ **SLADE** ▶▶▶▶▶▶▶▶▶▶
▶▶▶▶▶▶▶▶▶▶ ▶▶▶▶▶▶▶▶▶▶

"Mama Weer All Crazee Now" brüllte Noddy Holder im Herbst 1972 durch die deutschen Konzerthallen und vieltausendfach donnerte das "Yes" zurück. Mit Spiegelhüten, Ringelsocken und Lametta auf der Montur tobten sich Band und Fans gleichermaßen aus. Verrückte Zeiten. Nun sind sie wieder da: Slade sind zurück.

Auf dem Höhepunkt ihrer Popularität, Slade kreierten in knapp fünf Jahren 18 Hits nacheinander, hatte sich die Band nach Amerika verabschiedet. Sie gaben verschiedene Konzerte, sammelten neue Eindrücke in der aktuellen amerikanischen Musikszenerie und sind jetzt mit reichlich Rock im Kopf back in Europa.

| Deutsche Grammophon Gesellschaft mbH | 2000 Hamburg 36 Postfach 301240 Hohe Bleichen 14-16 | Ruf 040/35 96 1 Telex 2-163 923 | Abdruck honorarfrei Belege erbeten Rezensionsexemplare | Fotos und weitere Informationen auf Anfrage |

JANUARY 1977

The quite valid question was asked in Supersonic Magazine: Are Slade coming back?

ARE SLADE COMING BACK?

Q "Can you find out for me if Slade are ever coming back to Britain again! I miss them so much." *Carol Plummer, Crewe.*

A Slade are definitely going to return here, but when is not yet decided. They're busy showing America just how good they are, and since it's a huge country, that takes a long time. Sometimes a group with a hit record in one state have never sold a record in another. So they have to keep on pumping away until everyone knows them!

Little did many know it, but Slade were already back home.

They had seemingly given up on America, late on during 1976, as they had not got a chart hit or significant radio exposure during their stay, and the press regularly savaged them, or repeatedly stated their confusion as to why they were so loud and so English and why Noddy Holder insisted on getting stoned and disinterested audiences involved in the live shows. Dwindling resources had also partly dictated their return. The US stay was said later to have come out of their savings. No home tour dates were announced, and they weren't on TV, apart from the sparse promotion for their singles.

1977 would see the group starting their gradual climb back to some prominence in Britain.

And it was going to be quite a bit of a steep climb back. In their absence, a bunch of newer groups had emerged, arguably a whole lot less talented, but nevertheless getting catchy songs in the shops and with the right look for the kids magazines. Disco music and dance music had come to the fore.

Slade and partners

It was also the early years of punk rock. Punk rock was centred about the notion of not having to be a great player, but of *just getting up and doing it, regardless of ability*.

As much as people like to say that punk rock got rid of 'dinosaurs' and 'boring old farts' like Pink Floyd, The Eagles and Genesis with their 20 minute guitar solos, it didn't actually stamp them out. Punk didn't take over the charts in 1976. Many of the records were so bad that only John Peel would play them. The Sex Pistols first single, *Anarchy In The UK* managed to be withdrawn from shops quite quickly as EMI fell out with them over a disastrous TV appearance. Their second single, *God Save The Queen* was hastily withdrawn, because some of the 'old farts' on the new label had gone as far as to complain about them being signed to A&M! The *attitude* of punk did far more damage than the actual records sales. Most actual punk rock music didn't even get onto the radio.

New wave acts like Elvis Costello and The Attractions would start to dominate their share of the charts in 1977. The short, snappy pop song – with its topical lyrical message aimed right at the kids on the street - was coming back. That was what Slade now had to compete with.

Wednesday 12th - Recording "Supersonic" TV show.

The group performed what seemed to be a live version of their new single, Gypsy Roadhog.

Thursday 13th – The 'Rock Street' photo session takes place in London.

Saturday 15th - De Lane Lea Studio. Dean Street, London. - Recording.

Monday 17th - BBC Recording Gypsy Roadhog for Blue Peter.

Blue Peter

Noddy Holder would later tell Sky TV: *"The song was all about a cocaine dealer in America, but it was actually an anti-drug song. The next day in all the newspapers, Keith Richards had just been arrested for cocaine and there's all things in the paper about using silver spoons and everything. Blue Peter went berserk when they found out the song was about cocaine, 'cause it had already gone out then. Radio One banned the record and it sank without a trace."*

Blue Peter Producer Biddy Baxter had insisted on lyric changes for the TV show, and he didn't go screaming to the BBC about the original lyrics. The BBC didn't let the single onto the all-important Radio One playlist, effectively murdering it, as Radio One and Top Of The Pops was the epicentre of music promotion at that time.

Tuesday 18th - De Lane Lea Studio. Dean Street, London – Recording.

Wednesday 19th - BBC Centre, Wood Lane .London - Recording Top Of The Pops.

Top Of The Pops

Friday 21st: The release of Gypsy Roadhog / Forest Full Of Needles. Barn Records 2014 105.

Their Polydor deal had either ended or had been terminated. Chas Chandler took them to his own new label and Polydor distributed the records but had no involvement in plugging or advertising them. There are certain advantages to being signed to a major label.

A BBC ban on the record because of mentions of drugs in the lyrics hampered its chart progress somewhat, so it reached number 48 during its two week stay on the charts.

The British music press had remained reasonably respectful during 1976, but 1977 would be a different year for Slade. The press turned plain nasty on them. A new single was a perfect opportunity to get out the knives.

THE ONES THAT WON'T STICK TO THE WALL

SLADE 'Gypsy Roadhog' (Barn) This makes all the right sounds and even has a toe tapping beat, but if isn't a patch on the rude, offensive, and entirely wonderful noise these boys made some four or more years ago. It's careful use of American place names and general blandness could give them that desparately needed American hit, but as far as these isles are concerned, it's just the latest step in their continuing irrelevance.

Slade: "Gypsy Roadhog" (Barn). I once made the mistake of politely interviewing Noddy Holder and saying how much I liked his band, only to slam his latest single in print. He was furious and as a punishment, Chas Chandler promised to play me all the Slade hits one after another. He intended to prove to me how individual and different-sounding they all were. Unfortunately the demonstration never took place so, although I STILL fondly remember the band's past glories, I do seem to recall having heard this insistent than immediately memorable but McCafferty in full flood gives it the necessary distinction to raise it above average. Chart potential.

SLADE: 'Gypsy Roadhog' (Barn 2014 105). As subtle as a leg iron, the Wolverhampton Wanderers return to the fold and just as if there had been no musical progression in the last two years. They could be in the same league as Quo if they tidied up the sound. Cedric's ears quivered with excitement, a sensation hitherto reserved for William Wordsworth.
+ + +

SLADE: Gypsy Roadhog (Barn). A nondescript rocker, replete with lavish rhythm chording that completely lacks any finesse. Slade won't haul themselves back with stuff like this. Next.

Wednesday 26th
Advision Studio.
23 Gosfied Street, London
Recording "Ready Steady Kids"

Thursday 27th
Advision Studio.
23 Gosfield Street, London.

Bravo announced the good news that Noddy Holder had become a father.

"Hallo, BRAVO! Was ist mit den Slade los? Ich habe schon lange nichts von ihnen gehört!" fragt Kurt F. aus Villach/Österr. – Mitte Januar ist die neue Single der Slade „Gypsie Roadhog" auf den Markt gekommen. Noddy Holder wurde am 27. 12. '76 Vater eines Mädchens, das auf den Namen Charisse getauft wurde, Dave Hill hat in der Zwischenzeit auch geheiratet, seine Frau ist eine Friseuse und heißt Janice. Der einzige Junggeselle der Gruppe ist jetzt Don.

Mrs. Holder, Noddy, Baby Charisse

Other column inches came from slightly nonsensical stories like this:

If you've been wondering what Slade have been up to lately, the answer's skateboarding!
   At least Noddy Holder has been trying it out while the band have been in America.
   "Not too successfully, though," Noddy confessed. "I went too fast down a hill on one of my first outings.
   "I couldn't handle a bend in the road, and I went zooming up someone's driveway — straight into the place where all the dustbins were. There were bins and rubbish scattered all over the garden!"
   "The owner wasn't too pleased about it. Have you ever tried running away from someone when you've got a limp and feel like every bone in your body is broken?"

HOW NODDY GOT A DAMAGED BODY!

FEBRUARY 1977

British Top 50 Singles

1	1	DON'T GIVE UP ON US, David Soul	Private Stock
2	2	DON'T CRY FOR ME ARGENTINA, Julie Covington	MCA
3	3	SIDE SHOW, Barry Biggs	Dynamic
4	4	ISN'T SHE LOVELY, David Parton	Pye
5	15	WHEN I NEED YOU, Leo Sayer	Chrysalis
6	8	DADDY COOL, Boney M	Atlantic
7	5	YOU'RE MORE THAN A NUMBER, Drifters	Arista
8	7	THINGS WE DO FOR LOVE, 10cc	Mercury
9	13	SUSPICION, Elvis Presley	RCA
10	10	CAR WASH, Rose Royce	MCA
11	9	WILD SIDE OF LIFE, Status Quo	Vertigo
12	18	DON'T BELIEVE A WORD, Thin Lizzy	Vertigo
13	6	I WISH, Stevie Wonder	Tamla Motown
14	25	DON'T LEAVE ME THIS WAY, Harold Melvin & The Bluenotes	CBS
15	12	DR. LOVE, Tina Charles	CBS
16	28	JACK IN THE BOX, Moments	All Platinum
17	16	GRANDMA'S PARTY, Paul Nicholas	RSO
18	19	PORTSMOUTH, Mike Oldfield	Virgin
19	30	BOOGIE NIGHTS, Heatwave	GTO
20	23	NEW KID IN TOWN, Eagles	Asylum
21	38	SING ME, Brothers	Bus Stop
22	14	LIVING NEXT DOOR TO ALICE, Smokie	Rak
23	20	EVERYMAN MUST HAVE A DREAM, Liverpool Express	Warner Bros
24	11	UNDER THE MOON OF LOVE, Showaddywaddy	Arista
25	24	SMILE, Pussycat	Sonet
26	29	IT TAKES ALL NIGHT LONG, Gary Glitter	Arista
27	32	WHAT CAN I SAY, Boz Scaggs	CBS
28	47	EVERYBODY'S TALKIN' 'BOUT LOVE, Silver Convention	Magnet
29	-	MIGHTY POWER OF LOVE, Tavares	Capitol
30	37	MORE THAN A FEELING, Boston	Epic
31	26	FLIP, Jesse Green	EMI
32	42	WAKE UP SUSAN, Detroit Spinners	Atlantic
33	39	EVERY LITTLE TEARDROP, Gallagher & Lyle	A&M
34	17	MONEY MONEY MONEY, Abba	CBS
35	45	YEAR OF THE CAT, Al Stewart	RCA
36	27	LOST WITHOUT YOUR LOVE, Bread	Elektra
37	50	BODY HEAT, James Brown	Polydor
38	-	DON'T LEAVE ME THIS WAY, Thelma Houston	Motown
39	31	HAITIAN DIVORCE, Steely Dan	ABC
40	-	CHANSON D'AMOUR, Manhattan Transfer	Atlantic
41	49	I WANNA GO BACK, New Seekers	CBS
42	41	SHAKE YOUR RUMP TO THE FUNK, Bar-Kays	Mercury
43	43	YOU + ME — LOVE, Undisputed Truth	Warner Bros
44	-	DAZZ, Brick	Bang
45	48	SING ME AN OLD FASHIONED SONG, Billie Jo Spears	UA
46	-	HA CHA CHA, Brass Construction	United Artists
47	40	THE WRECK OF THE EDMUND FITZGERALD, Gordon Lightfoot	Reprise
48	-	GYPSY ROAD HOG, Slade	Barn
49	44	PUT YOUR MONEY WHERE WHERE YOUR MOUTH IS, Rose Royce	MCA
50	-	THIS IS TOMORROW, Bryan Ferry	Polydor

Record Mirror

Record Mirror apologetically tried to say Slade were at number 28 instead of being at number 48...

Monday 21st - Rehearsal.

Wednesday 23rd – Rehearsal

Thursday 24th - Rehearsal

MARCH 1977

SLADE BACK WITH TOUR AND ALBUM

SLADE return to Britain in May, after two years working in America. The band, whose new album is released this month, will be playing 11 concerts which climax with a show at LONDON Rainbow Theatre. Slade's last British tour ended at Liverpool Empire on May 5, 1975. They then went to the United States, where they have subsequently played 400 shows.

"We were fast becoming a parody of ourselves," Noddy Holder explained this week. "We needed a change. We didn't manage an American hit, but that wasn't the trigger mechanism for the trip."

The band begin their British tour at BRISTOL Colston Hall on May 1 and continue at BOURNEMOUTH Winter Gardens (2), SHEFFIELD City Hall (3), LIVERPOOL Empire (4), BIRMINGHAM Hippodrome (5), WOLVERHAMPTON Civic Hall (6), MANCHESTER Free Trade Hall (7), NEWCASTLE City Hall (8), GLASGOW Apollo (9), IPSWICH Gaumont (11) and LONDON Rainbow (12).

Their new album, called "Whatever Happened To Slade," is rush-released this month, although no date has yet been set.

SLADE
Tour and album

SLADE'S FIRST British tour for two years has been announced for May.

They open on May 1, at Bristol Colston Hall, then Bournemouth Winter Gardens 2, Sheffield City Hall 3, Liverpool Empire 4, Birmingham Hippodrome 5, Wolverhampton Civic Hall 6, Manchester Free Trade Hall 7, Newcastle City Hall 8, Glasgow Apollo 9, Ipswich Gaumont 11, London Rainbow 12.

Their new album 'Whatever Happened To Slade?' is released on April 21.

Wednesday 2nd
Rehearsal at Birmingham Hippodrome

Thursday 3rd – Rehearsal
Sunday 6th - Rehearsal

Monday 14th - Rehearsal

Tuesday 15th - Rehearsal Cannock

Wednesday 16th
Trident Studios. St Annes Court, London. Press day for Whatever Happened To Slade.

Thursday 17th
Recorded "Burning In The Heat of Love"

Saturday 19th
Birmingham Evening Mail.

Slade cum bak

SLADE return to the live British scene after an absence of two years in May. The band have a new album released later this month when they begin an extensive European tour which climaxes with 11 British concerts.

The album is called, appropriately, 'Whatever Happened To Slade?' and it's released on March 21, nearly a year after their previous record, 'Nobody's Fool'.

The British leg of their tour begins at Bristol Colston Hall on May 1 and continues at Bournemouth Winter Gardena 2, Sheffield City Hall 3, Liverpool Empire 4, Birmingham Hippodrome 5, Wolverhampton Civic Hall 6, Manchester Free Trade Hall 7, Newcastle City Hall 8, Glasgow Apollo 9, Ipswich Gaumont 11, London Rainbow 12.

Slade...back after two years.

Slade back with album and a tour

SLADE (remember them?) return to the British live recording scene after a two-year absence.

They have a new album set for later this month. And with a tongue-in-cheek irony, it's called "Whatever Happened To Slade?" It has been nearly a year since their last album "Nobody's Fools" was released.

The group have been attempting to further their career in America in the last two years.

They will play Birmingham Hippodrome on May 5 and Wolverhampton Civic Hall the following night.

Monday 21st - Mixing "Burning In The Heat of Love"

The new album 'Whatever Happened To Slade' is released on Barn Records 2314203.

Be / Lightning Never Strikes Twice / Gypsy Roadhog / Dogs Of Vengeance / When Fantasy Calls / One Eyed Jacks With Moustaches / Big Apple Blues / Dead Men Tell No Tales / She's Got The Lot / It Ain't Love, It Ain't Bad / The Soul, The Roll And The Motion.

The album was a lot more riff-based and had a much harder rock sound than recent albums. Another effect of their time in America, with bands like Aerosmith. It was a step back towards the more aggressive sound they had around the time of 1970's *Play It Loud*. That album only caught up on sales very gradually over many years.

It remains a hot favourite with Slade fans, although most would agree it was not made for the commercial radio plays it needed as it stood at that time. Was that a case of Slade saying *we have this music in us and we have to get it out and radio will just have to catch onto it?* Or was it what some of the press were saying - that they were out of touch?

The album did not chart, but to most fans that is the public's fault, not Slade's.

Only the ill-fated Gypsy Roadhog emerged as a single. Other tracks could have been good singles – the irresistibly funky *Be* was an instant hit with fans as soon as the album started, yet it never got a chance as a single. Neither did *Big Apple Blues*, which has often been slated as a fans choice.

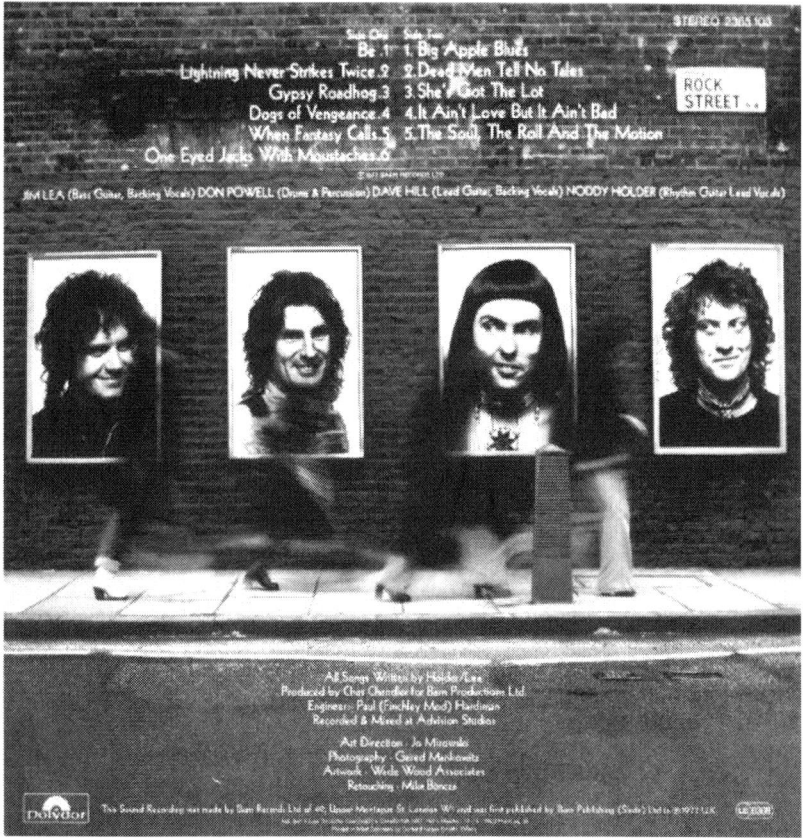

'Whatever Happened to Slade'

It's over a year since 'Nobody's Fools' was released, and nearly two years since Slade departed to the States. Anticipating the obvious question, they turned it into the title of an album that is guaranteed to instantly dispel any fears that Slade may either have lost any of their power or have changed their basic musical style during their stay across the ocean. Nod, Jim, Dave and Don are back with a vengeance. This is by far the heaviest album they have ever done, in terms of sheer rock force. Rather than spend months making a subtle studio album they have recorded eleven tracks with a totally live feel to them that shout at you from every line.

It's raw, it's earthy, there are no studio 'tricks' on it that can't be reproduced at a live gig by a sophisticated mixing desk. This is deliberate, because the boys want to be able to reproduce the numbers on stage exactly as you hear them on the album.

I said earlier that the band haven't changed. In essence, this is true. They haven't lost their gift for direct, blunt lyrics which get straight to the point — listen to 'The Soul, The Roll And The Motion' on Side 2 and you'll see what I mean!. Nod's vocals are, if anything, even more powerful and gutsy than ever and Dave's guitar effects have more than a touch of Jimmy Page about them. But the band, maybe as a result of their experiences in the States or maybe just because of a natural musical progression, DRIVE like hell. There's no let-up in the tempo, no slackening as the exhaustingly quick lyrics of 'Be' pile on the force relentlessly. They're tighter than ever, a fighting force to be reckoned with in a world of pretty melodies and too little musical aggro to get your rocks off to.

All the songs were written in America, and some of them stand out as having been obviously inspired by the place and the people. Yet they've managed to combine acute, detailed observations with a vintage Slade 'feel' that has survived ever since 'Get Down And Get With It' days.

"Big Apple Blues" is a song about the love-hate relationship you can have with a big, impersonal city, full of dirt, degradation and danger. To a stomping R & B rhythm, the dyrics portray New York's steamy summer heat, the jarring colours of yellow cabs, many-shaded people and blue-uniformed cops whose low-slung guns are reminiscent of the cowboys of old.

"She's Got The Lot" recreates the sexy hooker, the 'painted lady', so vividly that you can just picture her slinking into a pick-up joint, while "Dead Men Tell No Tales" is a Bonnie & Clyde type story about a bank heist, a movie theme drawn direct from America's over-dramatic daily life.

"Dogs of Vengeance" is a viciously heavy song that should be performed to evil, flickering red and green lighting to get the full effect from the violent lyrics and pounding music. Dave shows some great guitar work on this track, and also on "Lightning Never STrikes Twice", where his dirty, distorted guitar work definitely shows Dave at his best. The end of the latter song also displays some nifty reverb and panning effects on Nod's vocals.

"When Fantasy Calls" is a song which doesn't even attempt to hide what it's all about — the pleasures of the flesh! The lyrics are clever but not so slick and witty that the impact is lost. There aren't many people around capable of conveying down-to-earth words which hammer the message of a song streight home the way Slade can.

"One Eyed Jacks With Moustaches" is another number which seems to have sprung directly from watching people — this album isn't the first time the band have translated things they've seen into songs, of course. If you remember, "Gudbuy To Jane" also came from a flash of inspiration after seeing a spectacular chick wearing what she called her 'Forties Trip shoes'!

"One Eyed Jacks" is a series of portraits of typical American types, the fat, money-grabbing businessmen who Slade chirsten the 'bald headed eagles', the 'wide eyed madonnas' whose main asset is their face and figure, and the gigolos who surround them to try and share in their rise to fame and fortune, It's the whole fast-moving, ephemeral, materialistic side of American culture which is so beloved of novelists and movie-men — and Slade, coming naive and new to the American scene, observe it and capture in song.

So — whatever DID happen to Slade? They went, they saw, they came back and now they're going to conquer with this album, which is the msot confident, the most musically mature and the Slade-est thing they've ever done. If you've alsways dug the band, this is going to knock you dead. If you've go any friends who aren't Slade freaks, play it to them and they'll soon be convinced that Slade are the only band on the market to can fill the need for tight, driving, vital numbers, excellently performed, and direct and un-selfindulgent enough to allow anyone to become directly involved with both words and music. If anyone ever thought that Slade were just a 'good time band,' they're about to get their mind changed.

The promotional blurb signalled the end of Slade just being a good-time band....

Promo duties in West Bromwich.

Tuesday 22nd – Rehearsal

Wednesday 23rd - Rehearsal

Thursday 24th – Rehearsal

Saturday 26th: The new tour dates are advertised in the weeklies.

Sounds ran a lengthy rave album review written by Pete Makowski.

SLADE WERE PUNKS' CLAIM DENIED'.

'Remember the days when punk rockers were affable urchins who have thought no more of vomiting obscenities into the nation's living room than they would of leaving for a show without a spare pack of strings? Well, those days are back. Back in the highly acceptable form of Slade.'

This is what the biog says and what a load of crap!

If Slade are, or ever were a punk rock then John Denver is the next Messiah and Karen Carpenter was stand in for Linda Lovelace in 'Deep Throat'. And as for the obscenity bit, I vaguely remember a story about Slade in the early days when they were banned from a series of dates because they used 'blue humour' in their act.

OK, so they once had bog brush hair and attempted to project a skinhead image, but it didn't come off, so what's the point of a re-take on a campaign that's failed? Anyway, this is a bloody good album.

WHATEVER HAPPENED TO SLADE?

Well as far as I can work out, the band were always on form when they worked within the most basic of formats. Rock and Roll! Rock should be approached with a Neanderthal feel about it and these guys were one of the prime producers of commercially viable cranium crushing music. The singles were dumb but clever, almost manic in approach yet highly entertaining. But like all good formulas, Slade's volley of successful seven inchers came to a halt. They then tried for transition into more serious things, but failed miserably, basically because they were getting into things well out of their depth, they stopped sounding so cocksure and confident. Musically they're proficient, but somehow they sound more comfortable doin' the BIG BEAT.

The band have obviously been brushing up on their homework, since their self-imposed exile to the US of A. This album is high energy on a primeval scale. It's got all the ball bustin' riffs you'll find nestling comfortably alongside yer ZZ Tops and Nugents. The tracks run into each other, and it's got the same suicidal pace of the Aerosmith 'Rocks' album. Even though some of the chord changes are so old they're almost heading for retirement, none of it sounds blatantly derivative.

Basically, it's all down to the fact that Noddy Holder is a ridiculously fine rock and roll singer. When it comes to boogie, this guy's vocal chords are lethal. So powerful it's as if he's got a compressor implanted in his tonsils.

The rest of the band ain't dodos either. The drum and bass union of Don Powell and Jim Lea respectively, has a similar effect to a jack rabbit using your head as a practice pad. And I like Dave Hill's geetar, 'cause he knows his limitations and doesn't overstep the mark.

SLADE: *aren't dodos*

Eleven tracks in all, I haven't listened to the album enough to evaluate how long the initial impact will last. But it's packed with strong tunes, lotsa potential singles and the lyrical content is more interesting. I never knew that their single Gypsy Roadhog was about Rich Man's Marching Power.

The production is slightly flat, lacks the necessary sparkle. Basic and effective, producer and manager Chas Chandler has managed to capture and convey the live spirit of the band, but the overall sound lacks that trebly bite that people like Jack Douglas (Aerosmith / Patti Smith) manages to obtain.

Slade always reminded me of the Beatles at simplistic, gut level. Cold Turkey trekkin'. I mean, if the Fab Four have ever decided to go gonzoid heavy metal. Then this is what they might have sounded like.

Play it when your neighbours are getting on your case, it'll knock their Sunday dinner clean off the table.

Play it when your party starts getting paid back and people are asking for 'Don't Cry For Me Argentina'.

If you liked 'Get Down And Get With It' and the first album, pin back yer lugholes, no! staple them to the side of your head, now turn it up! Turn It Up! TURN IT UP!

Pete Makowski
Sounds

Record Mirror:

SAME OLD SLADE

If you ever spent an evening, way back in '72, sweating along with the raunchiest, sweatiest, rudest band in the land, you'll have the same fond memories of Slade as I do. The boys don't seem to have changed that much in five years – Noddy still looks like a leery, dirty old man, and Dave Hill still has that ridiculous hairdo. This is their comeback album – the one that'll make 'em or break 'em. It features their last single, 'Gypsy Roadhog', which didn't get too far in the charts, and most of the other tracks are in the same vein – solid, rocking numbers, but just not distinctive enough to make it in the same way as 'Cum On Feel The Noize' or 'Coz I Luv You' did. Part of the problem seems to be that they are trying too hard – laying everything on, instead of sticking with simplicity.

The result is that it all sounds, heavy, cluttered, even (dare I say it), a bit old-fashioned. Noddy's voice still sounds great and Dave turns in some pretty nifty guitar, but there's just too much of everything. In the old days, lyrics weren't too important to Slade, but now they're writing songs with Meaning – like 'Big Apple Blues', a song about New York where Noddy sings, "city walls standing tall if you fall, no one hears you call." But finishes up with "The apple ain't bad, it's just bruised and I'm glad that it's there at all." Or, on 'Dogs Of Vengeance' – "Come to my castle and I will unfold some exquisite passion so grand, some torment, the best in the land." Mmmm, all very well, but I prefer the real good ol' nudge and wink ditties like 'It Ain't Love But It Ain't Bad' – "Some of them one night stands, ooh ooh, that I've had. Keepin' me happy when I'm on my own. Keepin' me satisfied when I'm away from home."

At the moment Slade seem to be stuck between two fences... no longer making singles guaranteed to make the charts but not quite making it albums-wise either. Still their forte is really playing live, and I won't ever write them off until I've seen if they can still do it up there onstage. Rating? I'll give it +++

Sheila Prophet
Record Mirror

WHATEVER HAPPENED TO SLADE?, by Slade. Barn Records, 2314-103 (British Import).

It's an unfortunate fact that most Americans in the market for high-energy rock pass right over Slade without thinking twice. Unfortunate because I don't know of anybody who can pack more raw energy and confusion into a 12-inch lump of wax.

If it's any indication, for every gig they play in England, their home country, and where they are still most popular, they put aside at least $1,500 to pay for damages to the hall.

"They don't mean to break things," says Noddy Holder, lead singer and rhythm guitarist. "It's just the kids standing on the seats and jumping about."

The main reason Slade hasn't reached this kind of popularity in America is that they have trouble getting their music played on AM radio. Most radio stations consider them too loud for average audiences, but the band considers this ridiculous.

At any rate, their latest album definitely packs the kind of punch that would get that kind of reaction from a crowd of concert goers. Although it is fairly basic rock 'n roll, the British humor and sarcasm with which it is presented make it a refreshing change from some of the more bland sledgehammer rock groups dominant in America.

The best songs are "Be," "Gypsy Road Hog" and "Dogs Of Vengeance."

ONE of the biggest sellers this month is bound to be the new Slade album just released by Polydor.

"Whatever Happened To Slade?" is the unusual title and if the question really needs an answer one can only say that whatever happened is for the better.

The length of time the group has spent in America has obviously had a great influence on their music and their lives and this is evident in the music and lyrics of the eleven tracks.

There's a clever change of mood and tempo in this album, which includes the tuneful "Gypsy Roadhog," their last single which, perhaps curiously, was not the success the group had been hoping for.

The up-tempo "Be" and "Dead Men Don't Tell No Tales" stand out in this album. The latter has a catchy chorus and good instrumental effects.

The music is all fine, but some of the lyrics, especially in "The Soul, The Roll And The Motion" are really not for young, delicate ears.

SLADE
WHATEVER HAPPENED TO *SLADE]*
(Polydor)

God, if ever there was an album title which begged the question ...

The fished-for answer would probably be something like "Nuffing's happened to 'em, azzit, they're still GRITE," but the real-life reaction would more likely be a shrug and a muttered, "Dunno. What did happen to Slade, anyway?"

And the answer to that is, sadly, "Not a lot." Somehow, this album doesn't seem as if it's likely to change things.

It's loud, shrill and trebly and it sounds like Status Quo speeded up and stuck inside a large cardboard box. The songs are the standard stuff you get from bands who've worked a lot in the States: groupie songs, on-the-road songs and cutesy-cutesy-wiv-mah-silver spoon songs, plus hopeful stabs at Colourful Americana, all tricked out with occasional Beatley side trips and garageband guitar that's almost as terrible as the guitar on the first Stooges album but not nearly as good.

Slade were magnificent back in '72, but since then they've wasted their energy in unsuccessful attempts to crack the States; they've been away too long and they don't seem to be able to speak to the kid on the street '77 the way they talked to his/her '72 incarnation.

These days they sound hollow and thin. When can we expect Volume Two?

Charles Shaar Murray

APRIL 1977

Monday 4th – Rehearsal

Tuesday 5th – Rehearsal

Wednesday 6th – Rehearsal

Thursday 7th – Rehearsal

Friday 8th - Rehearsal

QUIET SLADE

A high-decibel Midlands group has been holding "hush-hush" rehearsals in Cannock Town Centre. Chart-topping "Slade" left Cannock last week after three months of top secret sessions. The Wolverhampton pop idols who had a string of hits in the early 70's, including "Cum on, Feel the Noize," were rehearsing for their first British tour for several years. They were also practising some new numbers before recording starts on their latest album. The group moved into the Forum in January and rehearsed there several days a week from 10 a.m. to 8 p.m.

Why did Slade choose the old Cannock Hippodrome, now renamed the Forum? Simply because they found the acoustics ideal. (Report from Jack Leighton).

Thursday 14th - Flew to Norway

Friday 15th – Nidarohallen. Oslo. Norway

Friday 15th – Burning In The Heat Of Love / Ready Steady Kids is released as a single on Barn Records 2014 106.

The A-side features a distinctive chord sequence and guitar riff reminiscent of The Kinks at their best. The drums are powerful and the song sounded like a hit. The B-side Ready Steady Kids is a good enough music track, but with slightly thrown-together lyrics. It sounded like they had written a B-side. Neither track was taken from the recent album. It did not get onto the UK charts. It would feature in their live shows for a while.

Slade get hotter

TO TIE-IN with their May tour, Slade issue a single 'Burning In The Heat Of Love' on April 7. The single and 'B' side are not included on their latest album.

SLADE: "Burning In The Heat Of Love" (Barn 2014106). First single in almost a year from Slade coincides with the release of their new album.

Sunday 17th – Kristiansand, Norway – Cancelled

Monday 18th – Chateau Neuf, Slemdalsveien 15, Oslo, Norway

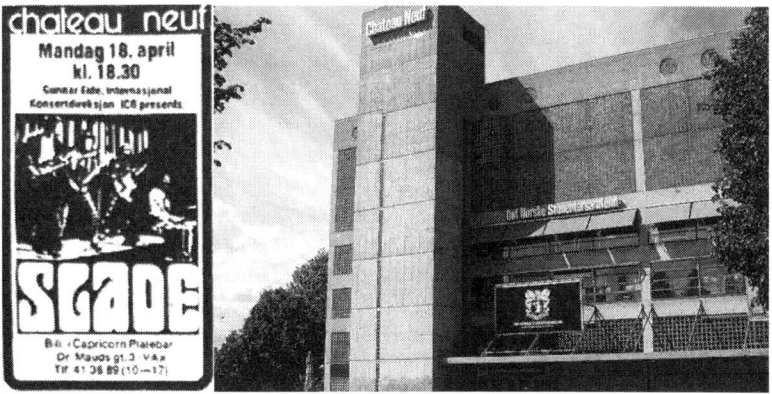

Wed 20th - Falkoner Teatret, Sylows Alle 13, Copenhagen.
Support: Mabel

Thursday 21st - Holstebrohallen - Holstebro, Denmark

Friday 22nd - Dyrskuehallen, Hjørring

Saturday 23rd -Tvedhallen ,Tved, Denmark

Sunday 24th - Aalborghallen .Aalborg, Denmark

Saturday 30th – *'FRAYED SLADE'* article in Record Mirror.
Sheila Prophet dozes off and finds herself on a trip with Slade in the land of Déjà Vu.

WHAT HAPPENED? WHERE AM I? *I must've dozed off and missed my stop. Last thing I remember, I was on the 73 to Marble Arch . . . and now, here I am in this funny street where the cars are all on the wrong side of the road. I know - I'll ask these kids over there. I wonder why they're all standing here, outside this hotel? They're dressed really strangely ... they're wearing tartan scarves and faded denims. Flared faded denims. And the boys have long hair - right down over their ears. You know, just like people used to have. They're speaking to each other in a language I don't understand. But there's one word I do recognise - a word they're repeating over and over again. The word is ... Slade.*

Oh, now it's all coming back to me. Of course - I'm in Copenhagen. I've come to see Slade. You remember Slade - they're the group who used to dress up in funny clothes and spell the names of their records wrong. They had lots of hits - remember 'Mama Weer All Crazee now' or 'Gudbuy To Jane' or 'Coz I Luv You'? Yes, you remember.

And here are Slade now, coming across the foyer of the hotel. Whatever happened to Slade? Why, nothing's happened to Slade. They're just the same as they ever were. There's Noddy, still looking like a dirty old man, and there's Dave Hill - you still can't see the join. It's just like old times - Slade are in the hotel, the kids are outside. It's as though the last two years never happened. But they did happen. Slade have been away a long time - for a very long time. And now they're trying to come back. Can they do it? They reckon they can.

Robots
"We really needed the lay off," says Don Powell, relaxing on a settee between me and the man from The Daily Mail. "We felt like robots. We'd reached a point where we just weren't furthering ourselves. At the time, we wondered if we were doing the right thing, but we had to do it." And so Slade headed off into the sunset. To America - the land of golden opportunities. It seemed a logical step for the band. They'd reached

deadlock on this side of the Atlantic. They'd been to the top - now there was nowhere to go but down.

"We needed the challenge," says Don. "We needed to go out there and fight." And at first it seemed they were winning. The reports sounded good. New York, LA, Boston. They were Slaying 'em.

Or were they? As time wore on, enthusiasm wore off. The reports grew smaller. Slade's blaze of glory was fizzling out fast. At least that's how it seemed this side of the Atlantic. But is it the truth? Don skirts the question neatly and talks about how America's given the band confidence.

So you don't think you made the wrong move? "No. It was something we had to do..."

On to the present day, and their tour. Don doesn't seem too worried about it all. "We're intrigued more than anything," *he says.* "We're just curious to see who turns up. So far, we've found a whole new set of kids coming along to see us. The older ones - the ones who used to like us - are still there, but we've gained new fans as well."

Don's hustled off to pose for a photo, and manager Chas Chandler starts to tell us how well the dates have gone so far. "Just like the old times," he says.

Don comes back and we chat about what it's like to come back after a lay off. "We haven't played live since last summer," he says. "It's the longest break we've ever had. We were itching to get back to work."

"The strangest thing was packing my suitcase, and going out to buy soap and toothpaste and all that. But now we're together again, it seems like we've never been away."

The new album is called 'Whatever happened to Slade?' Some would say the title's appropriate, even ominous. But Don's not worried: "It was a tongue-in-cheek thing," he says. "When we got back to England, that's what people kept saying to us, so we thought we'd use it on the album."

The press meeting is nearly over. The Swedish journalists have asked their questions. The band decide to leave for a sound check.

Mediocre
The hall is a 2000 seater in the middle of a shopping centre. Last time Slade were here, they packed out another hall twice the size. The support group is Mabel, Denmark's top pop group, made up of four blonde boys who all look strangely like Roger Taylor from Queen. They're mediocre.

We have some Carlsberg at 80p a bottle and chat to a Danish fan. He has the regulation straight, ear length blonde hair and a Slade scarf. He tells us he's paid 78 kroner for his ticket - almost £8. He likes Slade, but his friend prefers Abba. "I liked Slade," he says, "but they went away. They brought out no more records, and I found other people to like." Back inside the hall, the kids have massed at the front. There are no bouncers. The whole thing's like a local band at the school gym hall. The lights dim, and they clamber on seats and chant, 'We want Slade'. Yes, in English. That's Danish politeness for you.

And here are Slade - onstage for the first time since '75 and guess what? They don't look any different. Not a bit. Noddy has on a blue shiny suit and a funny hat. Dave is wearing shiny trousers and a wide grin.

The first three numbers are from the new album. The sound is terrible - a churning, muddy ear splitting noise. It's a relief when they break into 'Take Me Bak 'Ome' This is more like it . . . a good old piece of nostalgia.

Then it's 'Lightning Strikes Twice' - one of the stronger tracks on the album, partly because it highlights Noddy's voice, which is really one of the band's most distinctive assets.

It gets a good reception and they do 'How Does It Feel' from the 'Flame' album. And surprisingly, it works really well. For the first time you can hear every member of the group, including Jim on keyboards, and the melody line is strong and clear.

Then it's 'Everyday', another great slowie. It turns into a swaying sing-along, with the crowd waving their arms above their heads.

"This is the new single", says Noddy. "It'll be in your shops soon - so go out and buy it." It's a new song, 'Burning In The Heat Of Love' with the same riff as the Kinks 'You Really Got Me' and it sounds like a reasonable number. But really, it's not a patch on their old stuff - like 'Far Far Away' which follows it. It's the best song so far, without a doubt, with a melody that still has an instant appeal. If they released it now, would it still be a hit? I reckon it would.

For me, 'Everyday' and 'Far Far Away' are the highlights of the evening. From now on, it's downhill all the way. The next is 'Mama Weer All Crazee now', a reasonable rocker, but the sound's going again, and it soon degenerates into the same, thick mess they started with.

The Danish kids don't seem to mind - they wave their flags and their Slade scarves and beg for two encores. But I still can't help thinking what the British kids will make of it. Two years is a long time in the pop world. What worked then doesn't necessarily work now.

Since 1975, music has moved on, changed, developed. Slade haven't. It's as simple as that.

Reliving memories is fun ... for a while, but sooner or later, a band, no matter how big they once were, have to prove they can move with the times and produce something new. For Slade, that time is now.

At the dinner after the show, the band seem happy enough with the concert. But, as the night progresses, the talk drifts back to Wolverhampton, to the early days, to past glories. Those were the days.

But those weren't the days. THESE are the days ... right now. Surely memories aren't all that Slade have left?

Sheila Prophet for Record Mirror

On the very eve of the Slade UK tour, The Sun broke the news of Dave Hill's new hairstyle....

Or rather the sudden absence of a hairstyle. The Sun article still rather hopefully plugged their old single from January, which was now four months old, rather than their latest release – Burning In The Heat Of Love, which was a couple of weeks old.

Most of the fans didn't see the article and were utterly shocked when they saw the new look. The crop was more widely publicised after the Bristol show that opened the tour.

- **OUTRAGEOUS** pop star Dave Hill has slayed 'em again . . . this time Slade's flamboyant lead guitarist has driven his fans hairless by shaving his head.

- He became bored with his long hair and asked his ex-hairdresser wife Jan, to help him part with it.

- The group, who have a new single out called Gypsy Roadhog, start their new British tour at the Colston Hall, Bristol, tomorrow.

PICTURE BY DAVID STEEN

Pop idol Dave has a crack at being bald

IT seemed a cracking good idea at the time, as they say.

Dave Hill of the pop group Slade was simply boiling in the hot weather under his mop of long hair.

So he put all his eggs in one basket — and poached the Kojak look.

Dave's hairdresser wife Jan went to work on an egghead.

And this is the hair-raising result.

It's all chickenfeed to Dave, of course.

He's helped Slade to a top spot in the rock group pecking order, with a goggle of number one hits.

And no matter how he looks, he'll still rule the roost with his fans.

Even if he has to tone down the hairy rock numbers . . . for a little more eyebrow music.

HAIRY: The old Dave.

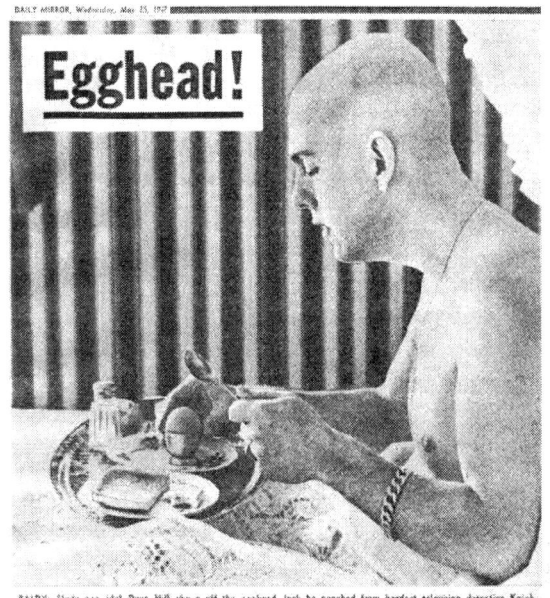

30th: Melody Maker report on European shows.

SLADE - ON THEIR WAY BACK OME

Copenhagen isn't, perhaps, at its best. They banned live sex shows here two and a half years ago, the Tivoli Gardens are still closed for the winter, the newspapers have been on strike here for over a month. And it keeps raining.

Over at the Plaza Hotel, there at least appears to be some sort of action. A handful of young girls have been hanging around, peering through the windows for much of the day, watching a steady flow of journalists, Scandinavian and British, go inside.

And inside, an impressive journalistic assault on the Plaza booze is interrupted by a raucous Wolverhampton voice, with a "Hiya, howyadoing", in greeting to the assembly, Ladies and gentlemen, Neville Holder.

Events of the last couple of years may have made it necessary to recap that Mr. Holder (or Noddy, if you're feeling matey) was once the unchallenged king of the castle. The brash and arrogant singer who sounded like he vigorously scraped his tonsils every day with a toilet brush, and held the precarious status of prime hero of teeny hearts through a commendable series of Slade hits.

Admittedly limited, Slade's misspelt titles, from "Coz I Luv You", and "Mama Weer All Crazee Now" to "Cum On Feel The Noize" and especially "Gudbuy T' Jane" made great rock 'n roll singles. Slade themselves exploited the loveable yob image for all it was worth, but they knew their time would come and they attempted to anticipate this fading of devotion and adapt accordingly. Their movie, Slade In Flame, though not entirely successful, was unluckily overshadowed by the inferior Stardust. And the first signs of slip from the throne became evident as their music mellowed; the ballads "Everyday' and "Far Far Away" were both top three singles, but "How Does It Feel" only made 15, and their most adventurous effort, the excellent "Thanks for The Memory", got to seven.

"Thanks for the Memory" came out in May, 1975 and the obvious conclusion of what transpired since is that the band made a conscious decision to sacrifice what appeared to be a leaking boat, in an all-or-nothing bid to crack the big one, the States. They haven't played in Britain for two years in their single minded concentration on America, and with the comparative failure of "Nobody's Fools" and the recent "Gipsy Roadhog" single, it's logical to assume that their once awesome following in Britain is now just a remnant. At the same time, they haven't made too much of an impression on America either. So it all looks a bit grim.

And so we are gathered in this hotel in Copenhagen for The Big Comeback. Slade, here as part of the build-up for their crucial British tour, saunter into the room as cocky as you like. If we expected any remorse or acknowledgement of tactical error, then we should have known better; only a band with of the most infinite gall would come right out and try to turn to advantage their own slip from prominence with an album titled "Whatever Happened To Slade?"

Later, with the excitement of journalists converging on Slade, the two never having had what you'd call a happy relationship, dies down, Dave Hill sits quietly in a corner talking with a fair degree of candour about the struggle they face. He accepts that they've blown it in Britain as far as a lot of people are concerned, but says they are all prepared for the fight back. As is evident later at the Falkon Theatre, they are basing their comeback on good old fashioned, rough edged rock 'n roll. Noddy's still the maniacal ranting vocalist, and Dave Hill, the arrogant, flash lead guitarist leaping on speaker stands, but musically, they've stripped all the decorations, and gone back to the barest roots.

It's said their gig at the London Rainbow is already a virtual sell out, but make no mistake, Slade are going to have trouble restoring their previous status if this gig's anything to go by. The new album is disappointing. Albums never were their strong point, compared to the excitement they produce live - but tonight the sound is terrible, the music relentless - lacking the vitality they've had in the past. Their outstanding history decrees that we give them a decent chance, but there's no way of getting around it - the question that arises is whether it may have been better to have gracefully quit, while out of the limelight.

Certainly Noddy Holder revealed sufficient character and flair in Flame to suggest he could develop into a personality figure beyond Slade.

Dave: "Sure, we got times when we down in America, but we never lost our sense of humour. We've always been able to laugh about a situation and we're not going to be too upset because we're not getting number one hits anymore. The Who, the Stones, bands like that, they've all had a dip at some stage in their career, but people don't remember that. Rock is now fighting its way back, but it's up against MOR music and disco music and all that It's the same situation there was years ago when Engelbert and Tom Jones came through with the ballads and all that slow stuff. I remember my Mum saying to me, 'Why can't your Noddy sing a song like Tom Jones?'"

Hill refuses to accept that they've been failures in the States. If nothing else he feels it's been therapeutic, a stiff new challenge after a run of success in this country, and while they're not disappointed not to have had a hit record, he's adamant that they shouldn't have done things in a different way. The situation has suffered as a result, that's undeniable, but number one hits don't last forever if you're Slade, the Beatles or Abba - and they had to move onto something else.

"We could have gone on churning out hit records forever. I remember when one of the singles came out and only made two and one of the jocks said, 'Oh well that's it they're finished,' just because it didn't get to the top. That's an impossible standard. But we haven't been together for 11 years for no reason - we had to do something new - a challenge. It was a real back to the roots thing in America, going on stage in jeans and tee shirts, turning up at the gig in an ordinary car and not a limousine and playing support to bands like Aerosmith, ZZ Top and Kiss. Support bands always get their arses kicked but we had to swallow our pride and stick with it. We've always worked against the odds - when we were skinheads nobody would book us. We've never done anything the easy way."

He even claims they got more kicks out of roughing it, for want of a better word, in the States. Maybe he has a fair point. Most of the supremo bands have yearnings to get back-to-basics from time to time, not just musically, and in the last two years Slade have been doing exactly what they'd been doing years before in England.

They were originators of football crowd symbolism, with an extraordinary close rapport and identification with their audience who, apart from the screaming weenies, tended to be the aggressive (though not offensive) yob, (a legacy, Hill thinks, of the skinhead image era).

Noddy, in particular, has suggested the good-time boozy mate, and the band has been consistently free of posing. So perhaps Hill's spoken affection for life at ground level is more than a euphemistic viewpoint of the struggle they've had. "People called us superstars, but we always thought that was rubbish. We couldn't understand people mobbing us.

We never thought of ourselves of anything more than working blokes. When we were sitting in a Rolls Royce and there were kids outside, it didn't feel right at all, we'd had felt much happier in a cheap car. We've never been super cool."

They made "Nobody's Fools" he says as an experiment. It was an attempt to broaden their scope to appeal in America, and was particularly aimed at getting American airplay. It didn't, and although he won't say as much, the suggestion is that he doesn't think too much of the album now. So they've gone back to being an out and out good old rock and roll band with no pretensions otherwise.

"Okay, we're arrogant performers and so on, but we've never flipped our lids. You've just got to follow your nose and we think most of the people in the audience just want a good night, a good experience. What's a good night out? Having a good time and pulling a bird. It's not sitting with your head between your legs and thinking, 'This is really cool', when it's really very boring. I've checked that all out and it IS boring. If you can't say it in a three minute song, you can't say it at all. It doesn't take half an hour to say it in a song. We've never been orchestrated or anything like that, but we did try a few things out on "Nobody's Fools" and what we are doing now is raving. Not a boogie band, but true rock. In the old days, people used to dress up like us, we don't expect that now and we don't necessarily expect to get hits again, but we're a good band on stage and when a kid spends his money coming to see us, he'll get value for money. Basically, we're a street band."

Much store seems to be made on the public's assumed desire to forgo the trimmings and get back to the basics, an attitude that's popularly in vogue right now. The most cynical might even suggest that they are attempting to ride back to the top of the new wave bandwagon; the old skinhead photos of the band appear on the cover of "Whatever Happened to Slade? might, at first glance, be the Clash or the Damned. Don Powell looks especially evil. By the same token the band's own ironic attitude towards punk is understandable.

"It always goes in circles like this. Like the Shadows getting to number one - Christ, I bought that album. Everybody wanted to play guitar like Hank Marvin. At one time the Shadows were uncool, but now it's all this nostalgia thing and it's cool to like them.

"I remember when echo chambers came in with the Shadows and all that, then the Beatles came in and blew it all out with very forward vocals, and that was the real thing. People didn't want a pretty vocal sound." As a fan of long standing (and suffered all manner of ridicule for admitting as much) I prayed Slade would turn on a good show during the evening. But even taking into account their stated aim to get back to street music, it was a dreadful concert.

The band sweated profusely and maintained a furious pace, but there was an element of desperation about it, not helped that much by the appalling sound, which obliterated much of even Noddy's terrifying vocals. The new album was there in force, naturally, but only "Lightning Never Strikes Twice" had any real impact. The kids dutifully called them back for three encores, but it didn't obscure the sad reality of the concert. Maybe it was just one of those nights, but I fear for them in England.

Colin Irwin
MELODY MAKER

Well, never mind if the music press were worried about the group.

At least the Duke of Edinburgh knew who they were...

PEN PALS

THE Duke of Edinburgh has won an unlikely ally in the person of Slade's toothy lead guitarist, Dave Hill.

" I read an article he wrote about what was wrong with Britain and I wrote to Buckingham Palace telling him how much I agreed with him," says Dave.

" He has just sent me a long charming letter back— and I was very impressed that he seemed to actually know a bit about Slade."

MAY 1977

MEL BUSH IN ASSOCIATION WITH BARN PRODUCTIONS PRESENTS

SLADE

PLUS SUPPORT

1st MAY	BRISTOL COLSTON HALL Tel. 0272 — 291768		6th MAY	WOLVERHAMPTON CIVIC HALL Tel. 0902 28482
2nd MAY	BOURNEMOUTH WINTER GARDENS Tel. 0202 26446		7th MAY	MANCHESTER FREE TRADE Tel. 061-834-0943
3rd MAY	SHEFFIELD CITY HALL Tel. 0742-27074		8th MAY	NEWCASTLE CITY HALL Tel. 0632 20007
4th MAY	LIVERPOOL EMPIRE Tel. 051 709 1555		9th MAY	GLASGOW APOLLO Tel. 041-332-6055
5th MAY	BIRMINGHAM HIPPODROME Tel. 021 622 2576		11th MAY	IPSWICH GAUMONT Tel. 0473 53641
			12th MAY	RAINBOW THEATRE Tel. 01-263-3140/8/9

ALL SHOWS COMMENCE 7.30p.m.
ALL TICKETS £1.00, £1.50, £2.00.

SLADE BOOKING FORM

To: Theatre.......................... Show Date..........................
Please send me................Tickets at £2.00 ....£1.50 ....£1.00
I enclose P.O./Cheque No....................... made payable to:
.... (name of Theatre) Totalling £..........................
I enclose stamped addressed envelope.
My Name ....
Address ....

Sunday 1st - Colston Hall. Colston Street, Bristol
Support: Liar

MEL BUSH IN ASSOCIATION WITH BARN PRODUCTIONS PRESENTS

SLADE

PLUS SUPPORT

1st MAY   BRISTOL COLSTON HALL

SHOW'S COMMENCE 7.30p.m.   ALL TICKETS £1.00, £1.50, £2.00.

It was noted that the singer from the support band Liar took a few snide verbal pot-shots at the headline band over the microphone at several of the shows on the tour. Perhaps they wanted to get kicked off the tour?

The Bristol audience were the first to see a shaven-headed Dave Hill appear under the spotlight, stage-left. Don Powell explained to Pink magazine that it was a shock to the rest of the group too. However, photographs were taken of his hair being cut off by his wife Jan. The very next day, they were in the press.

Guitarist Dave gives Slade a smoother look.

Slade's guitarist Dave Hill has given the group a "smooth" new image by adopting a clean-shaven Kojak look.

Dave decided his long dark hair should be lopped off to coincide with Slade's return to Britain. So he and his wife Janet set about the task at his Solihull home.

"She did all the clipping and I finished it off with an electric razor, he said.

"I did it before, in the days before we were famous. I was always the one who liked my hair short."

Dave's new bald appearance is not the only change of stage image for Slade. Their publicist, Mr. Les Perrin said "Their clothes are now more outrageous and extrovert than ever."

The group started their first British tour for two years last night.

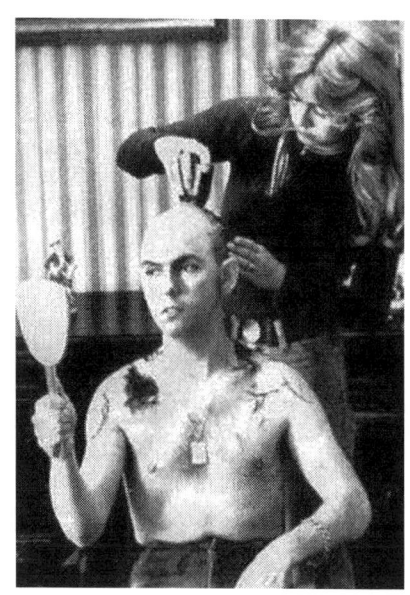

They played at Birmingham Hippodrome on Thursday and in their native Wolverhampton on Friday. The group have been in America for the last two years – but all of them still have houses in and around the Birmingham area.

David Gritten for Birmingham Evening Mail

WHO LOVES YA, DAVEY?

COR, it's enough to make even Kojak's hair stand on end!

Yep, it's Slade's very own Dave Hill showing a bald bonce and a coupla ears that'd make Dumbo go green with envy!

Actually, we reckon he's just slipped his wig off to give it a rinse – it's down there under the suds somewhere (or maybe on his chest!). Cor, what a lazy way to wash your hair!

(If we're gonna be truthful, we've gotta admit that Dave *really* has had all his hair cut off! His wife did it for him – an' I bet she wishes she hadn't!)

Monday 2nd: Winter Gardens. Exeter Road, Bournemouth
Support: Liar

Earlier they did a ticket giveaway event.

TIFFANY'S
present
Monday, May 2, 7.30-11.00
SLADE GIVE-A-WAY
You could win tickets for SLADE
Concert and meet SLADE in person.
Thursday, May 12
"STEVENSONS ROCKETS"
Admission 20p with this advert

Tuesday 3rd
Oval Hall. City Hall, Barkers Pool, Sheffield
Support: Liar

Hear Me Calling / Get On Up / Be / Take Me Back 'Ome / Lighting Never Strikes Twice / How Does It Feel / Everyday / The Soul The Roll And The Motion / Dave Hill Guitar Solo / Burning In The Heat Of Love / Far Far Away / Gudbuy T' Jane / Them Kinda Monkeys Can't Swing / Jim / Don solos / Mama Weer All Crazee Now / Get Down And Get With It

Strife for Slade

Slade
Sheffield City Hall

A PLEASANT time was not had by all at last night's Slade concert.

It was those little things which blemished the evening. Like the group's lead singer spitting on stage and spraying the audience with mouthfuls of beer.

Then there were the 20 or so smashed seats, bits of them thrown at the bouncers who were fighting a losing battle in trying to keep fans away from the group.

Before Slade appeared for their long-awaited return concert, scores of youngsters left their seats to swarm round the edge of the stage. Those who didn't had either to stand further back the hall or see nothing.

At times the stage looked more like a Monty Python set than a pop platform, with youngsters who'd managed to avoid the sweaty bouncers grappling with members of the group. Twice as the bouncers bounded over to remove fans there was total chaos as they collided with the performers.

First-aid volunteers treated eight teenagers who had fainted in the crush round the stage before being hauled past the group and out by a side door.

As far as the music was concerned there were no complaints. Slade played all their early hits, like Everyday, Gudbuy t' Jane, Far Far Away and How Does It Feel, plus a selection from their new album, Whatever Happened to Slade.

Sheffield was the group's third venue in their present 11-date tour. If last night was anything to go by, they'll be lucky to get out alive.

Wednesday 4th:
Empire Theatre. Lime St, Liverpool
Support: Liar

Thursday 5th
Hippodrome. Hurst Street, Birmingham
Support: Liar

Photos by Perry Bennett

Friday 6th - Civic Hall. North Street, Wolverhampton
Support: Liar

FUN FUN FUN AS SLADE ROCK 'OME.

"Welcum 'ome supa Slade" read the banner, waving precariously among the swaying, cheering crowd, as the Wolverhampton rockers made a triumphant return home. And it was as if they had never been away.

The whole audience was on its feet at the first chord, and on the seats by the third song, and they stayed there for the next hour and a half.

For Slade have one commodity that few bands possess - the ability to make people have fun. The music is fine - it's loud, beaty, and there is a wealth of hit material to choose from as well as the songs from their new album.

But it's not that that makes everyone jump around and smile so much, it's the intangible Slade charisma which makes everyone start enjoying themselves the minute the band walks on stage.

Of course it would be hard not to smile at Dave Hill with his completely shaven head, or Noddy, in his pirate hat and his knowing grin, as he sums up the audience. Dave, especially, with his guitar-hero poses and his ability to laugh at himself is enough to get the crowd going.

After that, the beat does the rest, and the old hits roll out to the cheers and waving and dancing of the crowd.

It really is a tonic to see everyone having so much fun, and it's only now that they've returned from America that we can see what British rock has been missing for the last two years. Because, although the act has changed in content, it still contains the basic ingredients to make people laugh and enjoy themselves. And that's a lot better than being spat upon by a punk rocker any day.

In support were Liar, a new band fronted by Wolverhampton singer Dave Burton, formerly of Fable.

JOHN OGDEN, EXPRESS & STAR

Saturday 7th - Free Trade Hall. Peter Street, Manchester
Support: Liar

Noizy Boyz back on UK track

Slade
MANCHESTER

I WAS ASLEEP when Liar came on. As the shrill thrusting boogie raked my eardrums and the vocalist sincerely grunted *"I've been up and I've been down/I've been lost and I've been found,"* I was paralysed by the type of fear usually associated with dark alleys and filed teeth. Not, I shivered, trying to rip my eyes open, the goddam Steve Gibbons Band again.

"We are Liar," said the ever so butch frontman at the conclusion of their five-minute bullying, and my eyes popped open in relief. Some relief... Believe this — Liar are a pale imitation of The Steve Gibbons Band, and actually played a song called "Born To Rock 'n' Roll".

A couple of coughs and a jump to the interval to scan the crowd: obviously predominantly male, a definite case of Whatever Happened To The Bootboys?, all eager to welcome the lads back into the fold. Slade had no one to impress.

But I reckon impartial onlookers would have been impressed, if not won over, by Slade's efficiently choreographed heavy metal — as slick as Bruce Forsyth and often equally irrepressible. The kind of streamlined powerhouse muzak Kiss strain for to accompany their visuals, not an ounce of flab.

On reflection, the band who gave us the definitive version of "Born To Be Wild" would probably be bound to return from a couple of years in the States so decisively disciplined.

Their set opened with three flawless, expertly constructed punches to the throat — all the right ingredients, the pauses, riffs, repetition, relentless dynamics, false endings... The crowd loved it, and were away and up.

It took a lot of the throng about this long to recover from the sight of a hairless Dave Hill who, with his Dumbo ears and Bugs Bunny teeth, looks less the grasshopper he'd been nicknamed by Noddy Holder than a cousin of Paulus the Woodgnome.

Only when Slade tried for finesse and pretended that they were a third-rate Beatles, playing trash like "How Does It Feel" and "Far Far Away", instead of consolidating their position as a second-rate Sweet, did things sag. Sophistication was never really Slade's forte.

Ah, the gross overstatement of "Burning In The Heat Of Love", the deranged indulgent guitar from Hill during "The Soul, The Roll And The Motion", the flashy bass licks from Jim Lea, and the formal pandemonium of Don Powell's drumming. Everything rehearsed to a T. Loved it.

Even "Gudbuy T'Jane" and "Mama Weer All Crazy Now" were transformed into gloriously anonymous, agreeably primitive heavy metal bursts, with Holder's mighty voice fitting (to understate) nicely into the controlled wall of noise.

Everyone had a solo spot three times over, the sound was perfect, lightshow spot-on, the crowd felt wanted and responded with glee. It was the kind of rock-as-showbiz outing that I'd pay money to see for years to come. You can't beat professionalism and precision when it's executed with such fervour. **Paul Morley**

NODDY HOLDER (above) and JIM LEA (below)

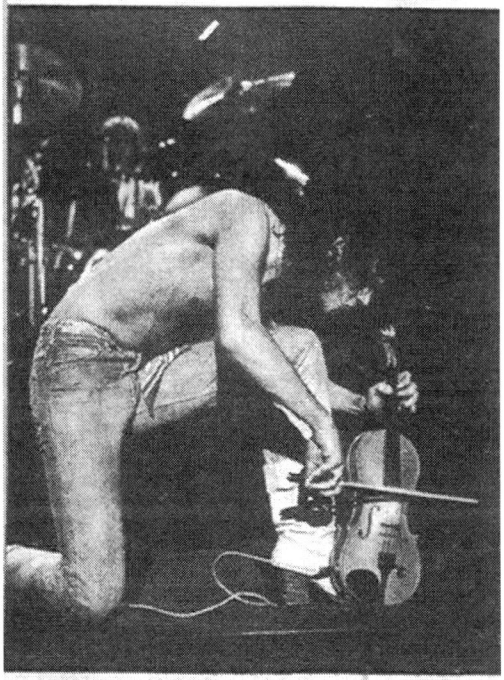

Pix: *DAVID STEEN*

This photo of the Free Trade Hall is not from the Slade concert.

WHAT A RECEPTION!

Travelling can always be a tricky business, but the lads in Slade reckon they have more than their fair share of trouble.

"I'll never forget the time we were going to a reception in Manchester," Noddy said. "Suddenly we came upon this big queue of traffic, and, just to make matters worse, it started raining.

"We were a bit late by that time, so instead of waiting in the queue, we drove over a traffic island! We almost made it, but by that time the ground was so wet our car got bogged down. There we were, in our dinner suits, all jumping up and down on the back of the car, trying to move it.

"Eventually," Noddy went on, "the police arrived. Instead of telling us off, as we thought they would, they actually helped us to push the car out of the mud!

"Have you ever been to a reception wearing a mud-coloured dinner suit?"

L. to R.: Dave, Jim, Don, Noddy.

Daily Mirror

THE LONELINESS OF THE LONG DISTANCE DRUMMER

This morning drumming star Don Powell, of the Slade group, most likely woke up in Manchester and wondered where he was – as he has done on countless mornings for nearly four years.

If it doesn't come to mind in a few minutes, a glance at his diary will tell him, He writes everything down.

Don has suffered from amnesia ever since his white Bentley ploughed into a wall in Wolverhampton in the early hours of July 4, 1973, after a nightclub party, killing his girlfriend, ex-beauty queen, Angela Morris, 20, and leaving him for dead.

His condition was thought to be so hopeless that he wasn't put into intensive care until two days after the crash. He improved with two months of treatment and slowly, and with difficulty, recovered his drumming prowess. But still he has no sense of taste or smell.

Secret
A few days ago Don, assisted by Slade colleague Noddy Holder and manager Chas Chandler, former Animals group star, revealed his secret to me – the first time they have ever talked about it for publication.

It is a subject they have strictly avoided; a subject that has plagued them and one of the reasons why Slade "went missing" in the United States during the next two years.

"Only we know how bad Don was after the accident," said Noddy.

"No-on expected him to live. Then, after a couple of months and he was getting well again. The doctors said the best thing would be to get him back on the road with the group. There was no escaping from the accident. Everyone wanted to talk about it. For our own and Don's benefit, we decided we would talk about the cash only when Don was fit enough."

Which they consider is now, on their first British tour for two years which began at Bristol last week. Tonight, they're at the Free Trade Hall in Manchester.

Verdict
Ironically, Don is unable to talk about the accident.
"I've still no idea what happened that night," he tells me.
He does not know if he or the girl who died was driving the Bentley. Both were thrown out of the car, and an open verdict was returned.

I America Don had two unsuccessful operations to try to restore his sense of taste and smell. They night return at some time, he was told.

"I can taste the extreme things like sugar and salt," he said, "but a sausage isn't any different to me from a piece of cheese."

Now 26, he has not married.
"I make dates of course," he says, "but sometimes I forget to keep them – or maybe three girls will turn up at the same time!"

Sid manager Chas Chandler: "I seriously wondered if he would ever be able to drum again. When eventually we found that he could, he had to learn things almost parrot fashion."

The group has had 17 hit singles, nine of which reached the number one slot. But for some time the buzz around the music business has been "Whatever happened to Slade?"

This is what - "And what better title for our new album than that question?" said Noddy Holder.

PATRICK DONCASTER
DAILY MIRROR

Saturday 7th – The NME run a feature on the previous month's European shows.

SLADE entering a room thronged with fans. Pic: PAUL CANTY

'AR THE KIDZ OWT'VE SITE?' SHOCK PROBE

Bands don't readily admit to being yesterday's heroes.. so Slade, not long ago one of Britain's most celebrated bands, will only acknowledge that they've been through a bad patch. **After two unsuccessful years in America they're unable to return as triumphant conquerors, but they're** *putting on an optimistic face and hoping to regain lost popularity with their new album and current British tour.*

And Polydor, who once boasted Slade as one of the best sellers on their roster, are not yet cutting their losses either. That's why they've invested more than £2,000 flying seven journalists to Copenhagen for a Slade concert and interviews.

Unfortunately, however, the facts can't be supressed. Noddy and Co's commercial decline started at the end of 75 when the single "In For A Penny" failed to enter the top ten. Two subsequent records followed a similar course, and then earlier this year "Gypsy Roadhog" only just scraped into the 40's.

In 1975 Slade could play the massive Earls Court stadium, yet now they'll be lucky to fill London's Rainbow. In a situation like this, the Copenhagen press relations gig is very important. Meaning, it's up to Slade to perform well. Sadly, they don't.

They play a mixture of their hits and album tracks, but the sound is appalling and it's rare to hear either Jim lea's bass lines or Don Powell's drumming over Dave Hill's exuberant guitar chopping. Essentially, the fun of their special clumping brand of unpretentious rock is missing. Noddy Holder sings well, but his usual onstage ribaldry is seldom evident, and no amount of gooning by Hill, the familiar glitter clown, can disguise a basic lack of enthusiasm.

Copenhagen's Falkoner Teatret (capacity 2,000) is only half full. We are, however assured that this is because the Danish papers are on strike and it's difficult to advertise. The night before Black Sabbath suffered a similar fate only attracting 1,100 people. But even so, Slade's third gig in eight months is a disaster, and at the splendid meal afterwards we all avoid having to speak to the band about it. Their disappointment shows, and the next day they're unexpectedly on our flight back to London, having cancelled three remaining Danish dates.

Holder says the papers will be on strike a little longer and he's reluctant to admit the circumstances of their withdrawal are within their control. Slade's strongest characteristic, in fact, is their refusal to submit to decline, although you might have assumed otherwise when they named the last album "Whatever Happened To Slade"

Jim Lea just chuckles good-humouredly over the title. He says it was tongue-in-cheek. According to him, Slade's misfortunes are by no means as great as they might seem.

With the sleeve featuring photos from their skinhead days as Ambrose Slade, Lea suggests that title merely alludes to the misconception people had that they were finished then, just as it's wrongly thought they're finished now.

I suggest that when Slade decided to quit Britain two years ago, presumably to concentrate on the American market, they were already slowly losing their commercial impetus. Perhaps that was a miscalculation on their part. Lea doesn't agree and instead argues that they had to leave the homeland because they had achieved as much as they could. Albums and singles went silver and gold, concerts sold out, they'd made the movie 'Flame', and then found themselves "getting stale, going over the same ground"

In fact, references to the group becoming "stale" are frequent. Going to America gave an opportunity to reflect on their musical prospects, away from pressure, and to escape from the inhibiting cocoon of superstardom and experience some hard graft as a support act.

"It was somewhere where nobody was putting the finger on us," he says. "You guys were all putting the finger on us and we ourselves felt we were getting a bit lost. It was more than just leaving England before we went over the hill. I don't think we even thought about that - because the records always went into the charts on the first day of release"

Perhaps that's true, but the entry positions were getting lower and lower. Anyway, in America Slade spent ten months on the road without having a hit, or becoming a major attraction (which seems like a protracted and ignominious way to consider their future).

Breaking America was unimportant, Lea declares rashly, adding that they didn't have any hits because their record company were not doing their job correctly. "You could say the material wasn't strong enough," he defends, "but it was a hit everywhere else. You could say it wasn't to the American's taste, but we've made a lot of different records.

NME

Sunday 8th - City Hall. Northumberland Road, Newcastle
Support: Liar

CITY HALL, NEWCASTLE
Sunday 8th May at 7.30 p.m.
Mel Bush presents

SLADE
IN CONCERT

Tickets: £2, £1.50 & £1 from CITY HALL
BOX OFFICE Tel. 20007. Open 10.30-5.30 p.m. daily

Slade
Newcastle

ONSTAGE, TWO thirty foot trucks worth of amps were stacked in a chrome and black wall across the back exactly and appropiately as for Ted Nugent. I'd come panting in half way through the first number, 'Hear Me Calling' and already the crowd was on their feet and yelling.

But poor old Slade have blown it, have they? Oh no. They hadn't got but a few bars into 'Get On Up' (from 'Nobody's Fools') before all the preconceptions had been laid waste by a band producing music from the premiere league of excitement. Noddy's Napoleon outfit and Dave Hill's newly kojaked bonce suggested the same old harmless pop gimmickry approach. The music suggested havoc. It was sensational: a riff as pile driving and anything Quo have produced with the distinctive fuzzed, rough texture of the Slade guitars and a hint of American funkiness working through. Compulsion.

I could hardly believe it. 'Be', from the new album, was next and it must be the most difficult thing they've ever attempted. The guitars said their piece, then Noddy and Jimmy Lea in miraculous unison tore through a tongue twisting lyric at impossible speed. A guy in front of me couldn't punch the air fast enough with one hand so he was throwing combinations. You just had to get it out like that or bellow something non-specific but appreciative: "Yah, Slade you motherfuckers!" Dynamics, dynamite.

These first three numbers were magnificent and the rest of the set, including some of the old hits, couldn't quite stay up there I felt. The crowd didn't agree with me though and neither did Noddy. They were on their feet and singing 'The Blaydon Races' while Noddy in total friendly rapport squawked away like a cross between Mr Punch and schnozzle Durante.

In fact, 'Goodbye To Jane' stood the test of relistening best, with its combination of speed, heavy rock compulsive hook line, full of ideas that they have developed further in their new material with 'Lightnin' Never Strikes Twice' and 'The Soul, The Roll of the Motion'. Their rhythms are still colossal and they have all come a distance as players. 'Lightnin'' especially on the revelation with Dave Hill's guitar harmonising with the vocal them Noddy counterpointing him on his own guitar. And this amid all that barmy excitement.

I expect Slade will be the Status Quo of 1987. — PHIL SUTCLIFFE.

It was actually a good review, but....

Slade simpers

"I EXPECT Slade will be the Status Quo of 1987" — Phil Sutcliffe, *Sounds*, 12.5.77.

Well Shitty, whoops! Sorry, Sutty, explain yourself you bastard. Last year you were reckoning they were about to come back (which isn't far to come as far as I'm concerned) now you tear bloody hell out of 'em. I saw them at Blackburn Cavendish and came back for more and more and more, they were brilliant child, the bouncers gave up after th' first half an hour. I saw a group of forty year olds twistin' to 'Gudbye t'Jane" in the aisles. Packed to the bloody brim it were on th' Saturday. They were all the ultimate power. Guitars on all fronts, playing stuff that could twat Quo any day. Jim's violin is not only different it's bloody unbeatable.
— **Slut, Gt Harwood, Blackburn.**

Don't get on the wrong side of *him*, obviously...

Monday 9th
Apollo. Renfield Street,
Glasgow, Scotland
Support: Liar

Wednesday 11th
Gaumont.
St Helens Street, Ipswich
Cancelled

Nod had a very bad throat, according to Don's Diary.

The show was rescheduled for the 28th of the month.

Thursday 12th
Rainbow Theatre,
Isledon Road,
London Support: Liar

As was customary, the Slade London show was reviewed in the next issues of the music press.

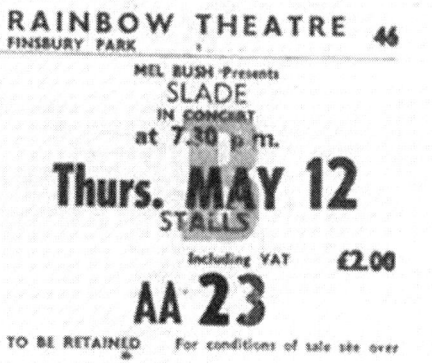

The show set list included:

Hair today

I HAVE just come back from a Slade concert at the Newcastle City Hall and they were excellent. The atmosphere was there from the minute they walked on the stage. The main shock of the night was when Dave Hill came on BALD.
John Patterson, Hetton-le-Hale, Houghton-le-Spring, Tyne and Wear.
● Gasp-shock-horror. Thank you too for your glowing review of the show.

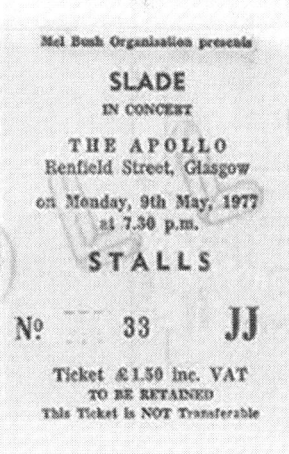

HEAR ME CALLING / GET ON UP / BE / LIGHNING NEVER STRIKES TWICE / TAKE ME BAK 'OME / THEM KINDA MONKEYS CAN'T SWING / EVERYDAY / FAR FAR AWAY / HOW DOES IT FEEL / BURNING IN THE HEAT OF LOVE / GYPSY ROADHOG / SWEET LITTLE ROCK'N'ROLLER / ONE EYED JACKS WITH MOUSTACHES / THE SOUL, THE ROLL AND THE MOTION / MAMA WEER ALL CRAZEE NOW / GUDBUY T'JANE / GET DOWN AND GET WITH IT / CUM ON FEEL THE NOIZE

It's good to have Kojak back

DAVE HILL: *you can't see the join*

SLADE
London

"'ELLO LONDON, we're Slade, do ya remember us?"

"Yes, yes, yes, yes!"

Crash crash, bang, straight into 'Hear Me Calling', the crowd are on their feet stomping and hollering. Idiot dancers surround me on all sides, I feel like an old age pensioner. Showers of dandruff cling to sweating bodies and Slade charge around the stage churning out a solid wall of sound.

I'm pinned to my seat stunned by it all, I just can't believe that this is happening. Perhaps I'm stuck in a time warp. The only thing missing is the glitter and the silly shoes, other than that nothing has changed. Slade are back and playing as if they had never been away, the kids lap up everything that is pushed out to them.

The new songs. 'Lightning Never Strikes Twice', 'Don't Wanna Give Up' mingle with the oldies 'Take Me Bak 'ome', 'How Does It Feel', 'Gudbuy T'Jane'.

It's just perfect, the lights are in complete synch with each song. One minute they glare and blind you, the next they are as subtle as a candle.

Noddy Holder stands stage centre leering at you making his usual comments. "I want you to give the girl next to you a good grope, come on a real good grope. Nice innit!" He controls the crowd as if he were a puppeteer, they make all the moves he wants them to without question and they love it.

Dave Hill stands to Holder's left with his newly shaved head glistening with sweat as he urges the kids to feel the noise.

"It's really great to be back, you've been lovely, here's an oldie but goldie for ya. It's called 'Mama We're All Crazy Now'.

Another cue for crazy dancing and this time the audience are gathered around the foot of the stage throbbing like a burnt wrist. Their bodies writhe and contort, every guy has an imaginary guitar in his hand and he follows every move that Dave Hill makes. The sound is loud but clear, every note that leaves each instrument tears into you.

Above it all Holder screams, "Crazy, crazy, crazy, we're all crazy now!" The noise stops, screams and whistles batter down on the group and they wave goodbye. NIGEL MORTON.

The Stage ran a review of the Rainbow show.

SLADE FACE HARD COMEBACK ROAD

AFTER a ridiculously long wait with no explanation as to why, support band LIAR managed to get on stage at the Rainbow last week in front of an understandably impatient audience of shrieking boppers. Unfortunately, the long wait did not justify the result: Liar are just another rock band with nothing distinctive about their material at all. Some of their set owed much to Status Quo in style, but thankfully, Status Quo got there first. I was glad to be sitting at the back of the circle (and at the Rainbow that's a long way away from the stage) as their set was pitched loud enough to kill any interest one might have had in technique or lyrics.

Another lengthy interlude and SLADE appeared. Noddy Napoleon Holder and Dave Kojak Hill are still belting out the same old tunes in their inimitable style, but the band seems to be floundering between a number of images and failing to adopt any one of them successfully. They're glam rock, heavy metal, punk and bubblegum all rolled into one and their comeback is promoting nothing new, save an LP which sounds much the same as the others. However, it was a spectacular affair and lighting at the Rainbow is always worth a look. Their old hits were well received, standards such as "Gudbuy T' Jane" and "Take Me Bak 'ome" reminding us that Slade really did have a lot going for them in the early '70s.

But there is no variation in their presentation — apart from the keyboard section on "How Does It Feel", their material is terribly monotonous and Slade fans may not be content with it a second time around; also, they are unlikely to attract many new followers.

CATHERINE COMERFORD

Friday 13th - Flew to Hamburg

Sat 14th Birmingham Evening Mail

IT'S SLADEMANIA!

ALONG WITH probably every other musical journalist, I had my misgivings about the reception Slade would get on their first British tour after such a long absence.

Of course they might have expected generous treatment in their home town of Wolverhampton, but they were as surprised as I was by the scenes of Slademania that greeted them.

A banner proclaimed "Welcum ome supa Slade," glazed-eyed grannies gripped the arms of their balcony seats and down below the packed audience defied the vain attempts of heavily-muscled ushers to restrain them and were on their feet thronging in front of the stage.

ENCORES

To their credit, the group did not insist on playing only their new material. The mixed the set with old favourites and had the fans, older now, but no less enthusiastic, singing along whenever they could. Chances of "Kojak" greeted the glittering shaven pate of Dave Hill (official nickname "Grasshopper") and record sleeves, toilet rolls, scarves and even a pink umbrella poured on to the stage.

"We're gonna have a good time," roared pirate-clad Noddy. And so it turned out. Two hours, five encores and hundreds of decibels later, an audience rendition of " You'll Never Walk Alone " that would have done credit to the Kop finally failed to bring back the band.

Slade are now off to Germany for a brief tour, but, as Dave confided to me, they intend to hit the road in Britain again as soon as they can.

Saturday 14th - Ernst-Merck Halle, Hamburg
Slade / Pussy Cat / Supermax / The Rubettes

Sunday 15th - Festhalle, Frankfurt
Slade / Pussy Cat / Supermax / The Rubettes

Tuesday 17th - Niedersachenhalle, Hannover-
Slade / Pussy Cat / Supermax / The Rubettes

Wednesday 18th May 1977 - Phillipshalle, Dusseldorf
Slade / Pussy Cat / Supermax / The Rubettes

Thursday 19th - Westfalenhalle, Dortmund
Slade / Pussy Cat / Supermax / The Rubettes

Friday 20th - Sportshalle , Koln
Slade / Pussy Cat / Supermax / The Rubettes

Saturday 21st -
Slade / Pussy Cat / Supermax / The Rubettes

Sunday 22nd -
Slade / Pussy Cat / Supermax / The Rubettes

The vast majority of the venues on this tour were quite huge halls, often also used for big sporting events with large capacities for huge crowds.

Sunday 22nd - Circus Krone , Munchen
Slade / Pussy Cat / Supermax / The Rubettes

Monday 23rd - Sporthalle, Boblingen, Stuttgart
Slade / Pussy Cat / Supermax / The Rubettes

Tuesday 24th – Bochum, Germany
Slade / Pussy Cat / Supermax / The Rubettes

Thursday 26th – Bochum, Germany
Slade / Pussy Cat / Supermax / The Rubettes

Saturday 28th -   Gaumont. St Helens Street, Ipswich (rearranged from 11th May) – Support: Cock Sparrer

**GAUMONT THEATRE
IPSWICH**
Telephone: 53641

STALLS

Row   Seat No.

L   30

SLADE

on stage
7.30 p.m.
WEDNESDAY, MAY 11, 1977
Admission £2.00

This portion to be retained

Printed by The Halesworth Press Limited

SLADE

"WHATEVER Happened To Slade" is the title of the group's latest album and Ipswich last Saturday night was given a pretty fair idea. The gut-thundering rock from the Wolverhampton lads had people at the Gaumont dancing in the aisles and two over-zealous fans were carried offstage in a night that the audience will not forget in a long time.

But just as they will look back at it with nostalgia, so did the fans only really respond to Slade's old favourites. "Cum On Feel The Noize," shouted Noddy Holder and the crowd roared back. "Mama Weer All Crazee Now," he screamed and they went wild.

But the music that the band has brought with them from their two year spell in the States left little impression. Dave "Grasshopper" Hill with his newly-shaved head leapt about the stage with Kung Fu agility. It was a pity that his guitar playing wasn't quite so nimble.

Twice he was allowed to prance about the stage, jumping on and off a platform performing over-long and incomprehensible solos. They added nothing to the tracks from the new album that the young fans were already having difficulties with.

But the stumbling block of the new music was soon forgotten when the fans were whipped up once again to stomp out the good old favourites and to demand the group back on stage for five encores. —
RICHARD CARTER

SLADE'S ALIVE - A JACKIE POP SPECIAL ON SLADE

If you saw the words, "Whatever Happened To Slade," emblazoned all over posters and record shops, you probably thought they'd gone missing! But of course it's the name of their latest album, and far from being lost, Slade are back, on the concert track, more determined than ever.

And when I went to see them recently, I was greeted by a rather Oriental-looking Dave Hill, who was smoothing down his bald head!

"What do you think of this ten?" he grinned, mischievously. "It's my new polished look. I got a bit bored with my old hairstyle so I had the lot chopped off. Noddy calls me 'Grasshopper' now, because he reckons I would qualify for a part in 'Kung Fu'!"

"I got it done for our latest tour," Dave continued. "I wasn't quite sure how it would go down with the fans, and after such a long time away, we didn't know what sort of a reception the group would get either. But we needn't have worried," he said. "This last tour has been terrific and it's great to know we haven't been forgotten."

Dave was interrupted by the arrival of Don and Jim, who patted 'Grasshopper' on the head and then settled down for a welcome cup of tea, or "black brew" as Dave called it!

Jim says that the audiences they have are always a surprise to him. "Most of the people who come to see us are guys, and they've been fans of ours right from the start. Sometimes it's a bit scary. We get guys coming up onto the stage, dancing and falling around. And some of them are really huge, with tattooed bodies and the like! But it's incredible being up on stage and watching how our fans react. Often we like to see them sitting back and enjoying the music, but other times they get really excited and that spurs us on. It's very much a two-way thing."

"In Newcastle we asked the audience what they'd like us to play, meaning one of our records, but some chap at the front stood up and called out 'Blaydon Races'! We just looked sort of shocked, I think, because we didn't know it, but he began to sing. We played along and then the whole audience joined in. It was great, just like being part of a huge team!"

At that moment, someone resembling Napoleon came along! It was Noddy dressed in his silk coat and three cornered hat, but minus his parrot!

"I did actually have one once," he said, "but it used to fall off my shoulder at rather odd moments. No it wasn't a real parrot, just a pretend Polly!"

"Dressing up like this is really good fun, though," he went on. "We haven't got the hard image that we used to have, and anyway, changes are good for us. When we get bored with one way of dressing we just go on to something else. But then I'm lucky, I suppose. I can wear any size or shape of hat and look good in it!"

Just to prove a point, he changed from Napoleon into Fred 'parrot-face' Davies by putting on a bowler hat!

"Actually, I think Noddy has this thing about parrots," Dave said. "But then again, he's always saying how good it would be to live in a grass hut, wearing grass trousers and fishing all day. A parrot sort of fits the mood, I suppose!"

It's true though, if Noddy had his way, he'd be off to Tahiti for a while, but at the moment that doesn't look very likely.

"We've got so many places to go and so many people to meet that any time off is impossible just yet." Don explained. "There is a plan for us to tour some of the holiday resorts, such as the Isle Of Man, so that could be fun. And that way our fans could have a holiday and come to see us at the same time. If I do get a chance, though, I'll take myself off to Majorca for a couple of weeks," he said. "I enjoy just lazing around and not bothering what time I have to eat or get up in the morning. That's what a holiday really means – just lying in the sun and watching life go by!"

"I did actually scare myself once, though. I lay in the sun for about a week and then spotted myself in a mirror. Do you know, I didn't recognise myself, I was so brown!"

It's doubtful if Don would get a sun tan in the Midlands, but he enjoys going back there, all the same.

"Going out with my old mates is great fun," he said. "It's the simple things that I like, whiling away the night over a couple of pints and old memories is just about perfect."

Don actually lives in London now – much to the consternation of his next door neighbour. "Sometimes I tend to play records rather too loudly," he said. "And one night I had some friends round for a meal and about three o'clock in the morning, someone rang my doorbell. I thought it was the police come to warn me about the noise and I was a bit hesitant about opening the door, but actually it was the chap from next door, dressed in his pyjamas and clutching a bottle of wine. He was really polite. All he said was 'I don't seem to be able to sleep tonight. Do you mind if I join you?' Ever since then we've been pretty good friends – in fact he drops in quite often now."

It's a good job Don's the friendly person he is, because he seems to have a great knack of landing himself in silly situations!

"There was one time last winter, when I went outside to look at the sky," he said. When it was time to go back inside, I discovered I'd locked myself out. It wouldn't have been so bad, but I was wearing a t-shirt and a pair of denim shorts! After a while, quite a crowd had gathered, all standing outside in the freezing cold, watching me trying to climb up my drainpipe, but it had been raining earlier on, and I just kept slipping down. In the end I smashed the window. I've done that quite a few times now. In fact the glazier is now a good friend of mine, too!"

And there's no doubt about it – Slade are certainly a smashing group!

JUNE 1977

Thursday 2nd – Advision. Listening to Gaumont Ipswich tapes.

Wednesday 8th June 1977 - Rehearsals – Cannock
Saturday 11th June 1977 – Rehearsals
Sunday 12th June - Isle of Man
Friday 17th June 1977 – Advision
Friday 24th June 1977 - Stuttgart - TV Show
Monday 27th June - Rehearsals – Cannock
Tuesday 28th June 1977 - Rehearsals – Cannock

JULY 1977

Friday 1st - Rehearsals - Cannock

Wednesday 6th - Rehearsals - Cannock

Thursday 7th - Advision Studio - Recording "Not Tonight Josephine"

Friday 8th - Advision Studio

Thursday 14th - Advision Studio

Bravo poster image:

AUGUST 1977

Monday 29th - Rehearsals - Cannock

Wednesday 31st - Advision Studio - Recording "My Baby Left Me"

SEPTEMBER / OCTOBER 1977

Monday 10th October:

SLADE OUT TO POP BACK INTO CHARTS

Slade have achieved the impossible... they've come back from the dead!

After two years of flops the band - who were transiently the most popular in Britain – have a hit on their hands again.

Called My Baby Left Me That's Alright Mama. The record looks set to break into the charts in the next few days.

Which will be a huge relief to the band's four members, who were beginning to believe that the critics who wrote them off as 25-year-old has-beens were right.

"The thing I hate most is when people come up to me in the pub and ask what happened to Slade," says bass player Jim Lea. "They all seem to think the four of us have made millions and now we are just sitting back and taking it easy. But nothing could be further from the truth. We've all been working harder than ever before. We want to get back to the top again and we're working flat out to do it."

Adds singer Noddy Holder: "We all really need this one to be a hit. We want to keep our stature as a world-class band – and you need top ten record to do that."

Outwardly, Slade appear to have little incentive to continue working. They all have new Rolls Royces or similar cars and all live in dream houses.

"But we have to pay very dearly for the privilege of living in England," says guitarist Dave Hill, wryly. "We have been caught in a vicious circle with the tax man at the centre. We can't afford to stop working because

we have to earn enough to pay off all the tax we owe from a few years back. And then next year, we'll have to earn more money to pay tax on the money we earned to pay off the previous tax. As soon as we stopped working we'd be down to selling our cars and houses to settle our tax bills," adds Dave.

The members of the group were all born in the Midlands. Holder at Walsall in 1950, Lea in Wolverhampton in 1952, Don Powell at Bilston in 1950 and Hill in Fleetcastle in 1952.

Earlier this month Sir William Pile, Chairman of the Inland Revenue, announced that he was attempting to nail 300 people for a total of £30 million in back taxes and Slade are firmly convinced that he has placed them at the top of his hit list.

"We are one of the few big bands who haven't fled the country," says Noddy. "The Inland Revenue go to extraordinary lengths to try to catch us out. Every interview we do s cut out and filed away if there is a reference to money. Like one interviewer estimated we had earned a million pounds the previous year and the Inland Revenue jumped straight on to us, asking why we hadn't declared all this money. Another time, somebody wrote a book about us in which they listed every gig we had done in our early years together. The tax man sent us a letter demanding to know exactly how much we had been paid for every single show."

Silly
"The situation is really silly. We spent a year in the States a while back and nearly every exiled musician over there seemed desperately homesick. The only thing that keeps them there is the fact that US tax is never more than 50 per cent. British tax goes up to 83 per cent – and even more under certain circumstances."

Adds Noddy: "If only the Government would cut tax to a more reasonable level they'd nearly all come home and they'd be happy to pump millions of pounds into this country's economy. Half of umpteen million pounds has to be better than 83 per cent of nothing. Surely any fool can see that?"

John Blake
London Evening News

Record Mirror ran a decent length feature on Slade.

BAK 'OME
Slade's Noddy Holder talks to JIM EVANS after their exile in the States.

'SLADE: alive and kickin''

WHATEVER HAPPENED to Slade? A good question and one that's still daubed over many a wall in London.

And the answer to the question: the band are very much alive and kicking and once again after a considerable period of absence, find themselves in the singles charts. To bring the Slade story up to date I'll hand you over to Noddy Holder, frontman and spokesman for the band.

Current work, activities? "We've done Top Of The Pops and we're working generally on promoting the new single, 'My Baby Left Me'.

And we're going through 12 hours of tapes for a live album — all stuff recorded on the last tour, in the States and in Europe.

"It'll be quite a mixture of material. "Slade Alive' really cracked us as an albums band and being a live band is what we're all about."

Until about nine months ago Slade hadn't been around the UK for some two years. In fact they had spent much of that two years working in self - imposed exile in the United States.

Parody

"After five world tours in five years we felt the band weren't improving. We were becoming a parody or ourselves and felt we needed to get away to revitalise. The States was the only place where we could do this.

"When we came back earlier this year we realised success would not be automatic. We'd have to work at it. The single before this one was not a hit. I saw Pete Townshend on the TV the other night and he was saying the Who went for two years without a hit — and then along came 'Tommy'.

"Sure, when we came back the music scene had changed a lot. We arrived back to witness the beginnings of punk and new wave — the revitalisation of rock music.

"It's exciting — some of the bands are rubbish and some are great, or going to be great. And some, like the Stranglers, are very original. And the Sex Pistols have their own mark, their own stamp.

"Many of them don't have their own distinctive sound, like when you turn on the radio you don't know immediately which band it is — they don't have identities of their own.

"Another good thing about the new wave is that it has brought the whole club circuit back into play. In the early seventies the clubs were dying out and the only way a band could get a break was by playing support on a major tour.

"But it's in the clubs where the groundwork comes in. And now the circuit's back it's dynamite and there are plenty of young bands coming through. It as to be healthy."

Overnight

And in the States?

"We played all over the country. Sometimes we'd be top of the bill, others third or appearing as special guests. We played with Frampton, Kiss, Ten Years After, Black Sabbath, all sorts, we even opened for Santana.

"You don't become a success overnight in the States. You have to work and work at it. Fleetwood Mac had been there for 10 years and Frampton for eight before they became as big as they are now. There's no telling.

"I remember when Frampton opened for us. Both Mac and Frampton deserve the success because they've stuck at it for years and years. It's such a big country and we've still got a lot of work to do there. Even if you do a 50-date tour you only take in one city in each state.

"Yes, I think in the States they accept things more on face value.

"Take somewhere like the Spectrum in Philadelphia. There you might get Aerosmith, James Taylor, Cat Stevens and the Allmans all appearing in one week — and a majority of the punters will go to and appreciate all the different kinds of music being played.

"They don't categorise so much over there. I mean, we once appeared on the same bill as King Crimson — we're as different to them as chalk from cheese — and we still went down a storm even though it was their audience."

So, how'd you feel when you came back to tour Britain after such a long absence?

"Obviously we were apprehensive as to whether we'd fill the halls, but we did — selling out two thirds of the venue.

"At some places we'd get five encores — and that never happened when we were at our height. The kids seemed to understand why we had to go away.

'People still dig the band. We really appreciate this and were chuffed to see the fruits or our hard graft. It was particularly pleasing when the kids came round the back to chat to us afterwards and show their appreciation."

Slade are a live band — "after being off the road for a while we get very bored. Playing live has always been what we've been about. We got our first hit through our live reputation, not through radio plays" — but like most bands they make no money out of touring.

"Ticket prices are sky - high now — that's another good thing about the new wave, kids can get to cheaper gigs in the clubs — and they have to be unfortunately.

"The cost of touring in Europe is so much no one makes a profit. With crew, trucking expenses, big lighting rig and big PA, promoters have to charge so much to cover expenses. It's not the fault of the groups."

Would Slade like to go back to the club circuit? "We'd love to, we were in our element in the clubs. You get the atmosphere and the rapport with the audience.

"In the bigger places you can't get this. Really, I suppose the ideally sized places we play are the two to three thousand capacity halls like the Rainbow but even there I feel some of the kids at the back are missing out. "And some of the places we **played in the States with Frampton were so big the people** at the back looked like small pins. Ad - libbing and gagging the audience just doesn't come off in those places."

And what else have Slade been up to of late?

Fortune

"We did some live TV in East Germany recently. They can't buy records and don't see many rock bands there but we went down really well. I'd like to get it together to play other Iron Curtain countries like Poland and Russia. I'd love to see Russia."

Would the band consider setting up permanent home in the USA?

"Never we're paying a fortune in come tax but nothing, no amount of money can compensate for not seeing your family, not being able to have a pint or two in the pub with your mates.

"But the system here is crazy. We work for the taxman, getting 17p in the pound. In the States the top rate in income tax is 50 per cent. If they made it like that here all the exiles would come back and think of all the dollars that would come into the country.

The Government, the country, everybody would be better off. I just don't understand the thinking behind the present system.

"It's come to a funny situation when you're earning too much to live in the country where you were born. But we're not leaving. Listen to the 'B' side of our current single, 'OHMS' — it says it all about the tax system and the homesick exiles."

Slade are alive and kickin' and plan to be around together for a long time yet.

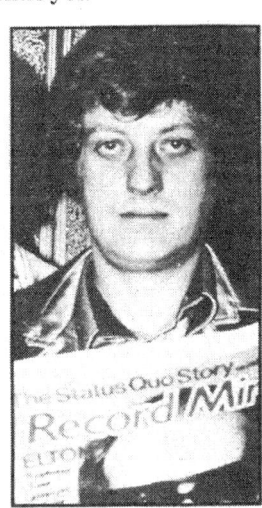

NODDY HOLDER: back to best

Friday 14th: My Baby Left Me But That's Alright Mama / OHMS
Barn 2014 114.

Elvis Presley had died not long before and someone came up with the idea of re-working two of his hits as a medley. It was a well-arranged and recorded version, despite the absence of Dave Hill on guitar. Jim Lea ably covered the lead guitar duties in his absence.

The excellent single cover image was taken by Gered Mankowitz. The single reached a height of number 32.

Released that same week:
ABBA – THE NAME OF THE GAME
THE DAMNED – PROBLEM CHILD
QUEEN – WE ARE THE CHAMPIONS / WE WILL ROCK YOU
SEC PISTOLS – HOLIDAYS IN THE SUN
TOM ROBINSON BAND – 2468 MOTORWAY
XTC – 3D EP

O T H ER RECORDS

SLADE: 'My Baby Left Me/That's Alright Mama' (Barn 2014114). A Slade slug at a Crudup past. Real pleasant it is too. But I can remember a time when Slade records were vixen fearsome rather than pleasant. Fearsome on their own songs, not some cruising rocker from way back. Get out while the going's bad. 'Cos it's only going to get hideous.

Grovelling twit

RIGHT. WHERE'S the so-called twit Barry Cain who reviewed the Slade single? What a sick joke you big, detestable lump. We know the boize have been having a tough time but they're BAK (man) with this new single
Mike and Linda, Morayshire, Scotland.
●Don't give the lad such a hard time you lot. It's the first time he's reviewed two records in a week for ages.

The review even got a review.

BEST COMEBACK SINGLE

Fabulous treatment of this old Arthur Crudup number could easily see Slade back in the charts. It's a bouncy, struttin' 12-bar blues quite unlike most of the band's earlier singles and it could be just the right thing to get them back into favour at the current time. On the other hand it could be that its remarkable similarity to the treatments of old blues numbers by a certain Johnny Winter Esq is clouding my judgement. We'll have to wait and see.

UK SINGLES

1	1	NAME OF THE GAME, Abba	Epic
2	6	WE ARE THE CHAMPIONS, Queen	EMI
3	4	ROCKIN' ALL OVER THE WORLD, Status Quo	Vertigo
4	2	YES SIR I CAN BOOGIE, Baccara	RCA
5	5	2, 4, 6, 8, MOTORWAY, Tom Robinson Band	EMI
6	3	YOU'RE IN MY HEART, Rod Stewart	Riva
7	14	LIVE IN TROUBLE, Barron Knights	Epic
8	17	DANCIN' PARTY, Showaddywaddy	Arista
9	12	HOW DEEP IS YOUR LOVE, Bee Gees	RSO
10	9	CALLING OCCUPANTS, Carpenters	A&M
11	10	NEEDLES & PINS, Smokie	Rak
12	7	BLACK IS BLACK, La Belle Epoque	Harvest
13	11	VIRGINIA PLAIN, Roxy Music	Polydor
14	21	DADDY COOL, Darts	Magnet
15	16	LOVE HURTS ETC., Nazareth	Mountain
16	18	SHE'S NOT THERE, Santana	CBS
17	13	HOLIDAYS IN THE SUN, Sex Pistols	Virgin
18	19	FROM HERE TO ETERNITY, Giorgio	Oasis
19	8	BLACK BETTY, Ram Jam	Epic
20	23	I BELIEVE YOU, Dorothy Moore	Epic
21	22	BELFAST, Boney M	Atlantic
22	29	I WILL, Ruby Winters	Creole
23	31	EGYPTIAN REGGAE, Jonathan Richman	Beserkey
24	24	TURN TO STONE, Electric Light Orchestra	Jet
25	25	HEROES, David Bowie	RCA
26	33	WATCHIN' THE DETECTIVES, Elvis Costello	Stiff
27	15	SILVER LADY, David Soul	Private Stock
28	30	GOIN' PLACES, Jacksons	Epic
29	20	STAR WARS THEME, Meco	RCA
30	50	FLORAL DANCE, Brighouse Rastrick Band	Logo
31	35	DON'T IT MAKE MY BROWN EYES BLUE, Crystal Gayle	UA
32	45	BABY BABY MY LOVE IS ALL FOR YOU, Deniece Williams	CBS
33	39	CAPTAIN KREMMEN, Kenny Everett/Mike Vickers	DJM
34	43	LOVE OF MY LIFE, Dooleys	GTO
35	26	LOVE BUG, Tina Charles	CBS
36	46	MODERN WORLD, Jam	Polydor
37	27	NO MORE HEROES, Stranglers	United Artists
38	40	SHOO DOO FU FU OOH, Lenny Williams	ABC
39	48	GEORGINA BAILEY, Noosha Fox	GTO
40	32	MY BABY LEFT ME, Slade	Barn
41	42	BABY WHAT A BIG SURPRISE, Chicago	CBS
42	—	(YOU'RE) FABULOUS BABE, Kenny Williams	Decca
43	—	ONLY THE STRONG SURVIVE, Billy Paul	Philadelphia
44	—	MARY OF THE FOURTH FORM, Boomtown Rats	Ensign
45	44	DON'T LET ME BE MISUNDERSTOOD, Santa Esmeralda	Philips
46	—	WHITE PUNKS ON DOPE, Tubes	A&M
47	47	DISCOBEATLEMANIA, DBM	Atlantic
48	—	MULL OF KINTYRE / GIRLS SCHOOL, Wings	Parlophone
49	—	GETTIN' READY FOR LOVE, Diana Ross	Motown
50	—	YOU'VE LOST THAT LOVIN' FEELIN', Righteous Bros	Spector

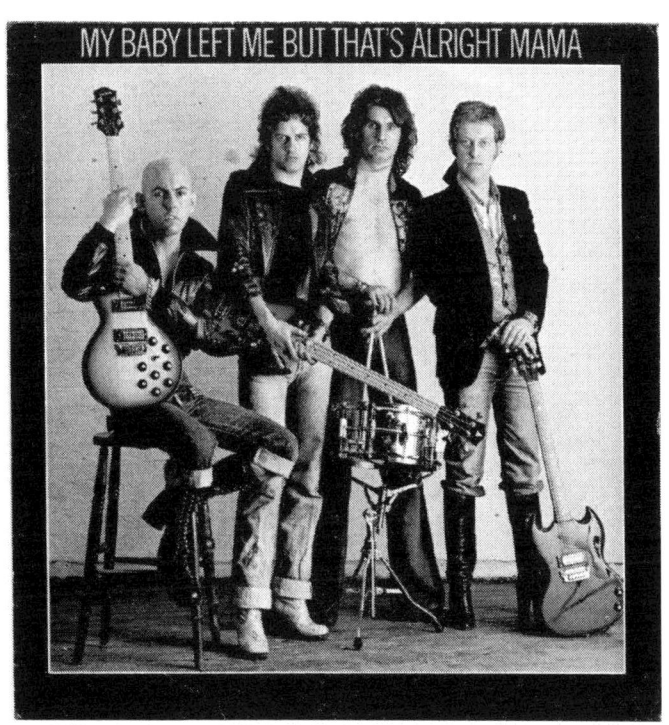

Friday 21st - Rehearsals – Cannock

Wednesday 26th - BBC, Wood Lane Slade mime to My Baby Left Me on Top Of The Pops. Jim accidentally knock the microphone that he is sharing with Dave off its stand and they still sing as if it was still there, while laughing out loud. A pure Slade moment.

● **SLADE: "My Baby Left Me But That's Alright Mama" (Barn).** Undaunted, Slade continue their struggle for re-acceptance. This won't clinch it. Two Arthur Crudup classics are knitted together in flat fashion. Noise rules OK.

SLADE: My Baby Left Me / That's Alright Mama (Barn). A determinedly hardassed medley of Arthur Crudup's Greatest Hits (both of them) as recorded by Elvin Preston — well, that's what Arthur usedta call him anyway. Judging by the pic sleeve their New Image (short hair, levver jackets, Dave 'Ill with a shaven dome etc) is great above the knees, but the silly boots and Don Powell's ultraflare jeans rather spoil the effect. Liable to offend Teds, punx, oldtime Slade fans and members of the general public in roughly equal proportions. A for taste, A for effort.

Agony of Slade star Don in fight with fear

MERCURY EXCLUSIVE

THE secret anguish that has haunted the Midland pop group Slade and helped force them out of the limelight was revealed for the first time last night.

Don Powell, the drummer with the Wolverhampton group who became international idols, told how the car crash in which his girl friend died and he was seriously injured so disabled him that it lead to four years of fear and mental torment and brought him to the brink of ending his career.

But the 28-year-old drummer also spoke of the care, consideration and encouragement of the other members of the group that gave him the strength to continue and their refusal to accept that he should be replaced.

Hidden prompt card

Unknown to hundreds of thousands of Slade fans, Powell still has no sense of taste or smell and his memory is still so defective that he has to keep a day to day diary of everything he does or must do. And when playing in public he keeps a hidden "prompt card" on the back of his drums to tell him what to play next.

The crash that began the problems came in July, 1973, when Slade were riding a wave of world-wide popularity. Powell's white Bentley hit a wall in Compton Road, Wolverhampton. He was thrown through the windscreen and into the roadway and his 20-year-old girl-friend, Angela Morris, was killed.

After weeks in hospital fans thought he had fully recovered from the ordeal, particularly when he joined other members of the group in a move to America.

But slowly the stars whose success had been compared with that of the Beatles sank from their number one slot.

Now back in the Midlands rehearsing for a British comeback based on the success of their new recording of the rock and roll standard "My Baby Left Me", Don Powell told me the real story of the last years.

"When I started playing again I suddenly found I could not remember our hit records," he said.

Daily diary

The trouble is I cannot remember things from one day to the next. I have to keep a diary of what I do and have to do otherwise I just cannot remember what happened yesterday or what I should be doing tomorrow.

"When I wake up in the mornings I just do not know where I am.

In the beginning it was very frightening I would get really scared. And added to that I have no sense of taste or smell at all. If I close my eyes I have no idea what I am eating.

"At one time things got so bad. I was so worried and frustrated that I really did think I ought to pack in playing with Slade. I could see no way of going on."

And in the pop world there were pressures on the rest of the group to "ditch" Powell because of his incapacities. But they stood by him.

"It would have been so easy for them to get rid of me," said Powell. "It happens all the time in this business. But the lads were fantastic. They stood by me.

"Now after all this time, I have learned to live with my problems and suddenly everything is starting to happen to us again. It is just as exciting as it was when it first happened to us. The new record is in the charts and we are now rehearsing for the comeback."

● DON POWELL, star with memory problems, says: "At one time I thought I ought to pack it all in, but the lads kept me going. They were fantastic."

NOVEMBER 1977

Tuesday 29th November - Pebble Mill Birmingham
Wednesday 30th - Pebble Mill Birmingham

DECEMBER 1977

Thursday 1st December - Pebble Mill Birmingham
Wednesday 7th - Munich TV Show rehearsal
Thursday 8th - Munich - TV show recording
Thursday 15th - Advision Studio. Gosfield Street, London
Friday 16th - Advision Studio. Gosfield Street, London
Monday 19th - Advision Studio. Gosfield Street, London
Wednesday 21st - Advision Studio. Gosfield Street, London

JUNGLE DRUMS

Don Powell, drummer with Slade, can't wait for Boxing Day, because that's when he usually goes for an annual treat...

"I take myself off to the cinema and spend the afternoon wading through a bag of popcorn and generally enjoying myself.

"Last year I went to see 'Jungle Book'! It's my favourite film and although it was the umpteenth time I've seen it, I couldn't wait to get into the cinema." Don says.

"The only trouble was, it was a children's matinee performance, and I must admit people kept staring at me. At first I kept wondering why, but as I was about two feet taller than everyone else, I suppose it was quite understandable.

"Also I did have my face to the wall, partly because I didn't want to be noticed, and partly because I was so embarrassed, but in a way that must have looked even more conspicuous!"

Left to right: Noddy, Jim, Dave and Don.

JANUARY 1978

WHY SLADE DROPPED OUT

THE Slade pop group sacrificed their careers out of loyalty to drummer Don Powell.

Don was very badly hurt in the car crash in which his girl friend died. He suffered brain injuries from which it took him a long time to recover.

For months afterwards he used to walk round with a notebook in his pocket noting down everything that happened or was said to him just so that he could remember it the next day.

He told the rest of the boys that he just couldn't go on with the band but they refused to bring in a replacement. Their attitude was that it was Don or no one.

In the end, they decided they would go to America and keep out of the way until he was fit enough to start working again.

The trouble is that pop fans are fickle, particularly the teenyboppers who followed Slade. By the time they came back it was too late. They have never had a hit since.

1st: Chas Chandler was featured an ITV show, sharing his thoughts on the punk scene.

3rd: Advision Recording Studio.

4th: Advision Recording Studio.

5th: Advision Recording Studio.

6th: Don Powell went to Harry's for a haircut

7th: Nod and Don went to 'Rags' to eat along with Brian May and his then wife, Chrissie.

10th: Advision Recording Studio.

11th: Advision Recording Studio. Don later went to watch a band called Sparrow (who had won on the 'Opportunity Knocks TV talent show. Don got up and played "Stagger Lee" and some other old rock stuff.

12th: Don Powell at the Speakeasy (Margaret St, London, W1) with Phil Lynott and Gary Moore.

13th: Advision Recording Studio.

16th: Advision Recording Studio

17th: Advision Recording Studio. John 'Rabbitt Brundrick' added piano to the tracks.

18th: Advision Recording Studio.

19th: Don Powell went to a Be Bop Deluxe show. They were recording "In Concert" for the BBC.

24th: Don spoke to 'H'. He'd just moved to a new house in Albrighton. Don signed the sale forms for his flat in Wolverhampton.....

29th: Rehearsals

30th: Advision Recording Studio. Slade recorded a first version of "Give Us A Goal".

31st: Advision Recording Studio. Slade re-recorded "Give Us A Goal".
The engineer put the drums in the corridor for this take.

SLADE

FEBRUARY 1978

1st: Advision Recording Studio.
H came down from Wolverhampton to record his guitar on "Give Us A Goal".

2nd: Advision Recording Studio.

6th: Cannock for rehearsals.
7th: Cannock for rehearsals.
8th: Cannock for rehearsals.

9th:
Don's diary: *"I was up at 06:30am - Swinn picked me up to drive to Brighton to film the promo video for "Give Us A Goal". Drove back to London and watched TOTP's with ELO, Dusty Springfield, Stranglers and Brotherhood Of Man."*

Saturday 11th - Brighton Football Ground. Old Shoreham Road, Hove – making the "Give Us A Goal" Promo film

Don's diary: *"I was up at 06:00am cleaned up and waited for H and Jim to arrive from Wolverhampton. We all drove to Brighton to spend the day filming at the football ground again..... I drove back to Wolverhampton with everyone."*

The match programme cover.
Score: 2-1 to Brighton and Hove Albion

SLADE
at the GOLDSTONE

On a bitterly cold day prior to the start of the Burnley match a crescendo of sound hit the Goldstone as 'Slade' launched into their latest single 'Give us a Goal'. All the fans in the North Stand entered into the spirit of the promotion and BBC South televised both the Group playing and the Crowd's 'assistance'.

Doubtless the film will appear shortly on 'Top of the Pops' and the Albion will have entered yet another field. The urge to 'Give us a Goal' could become a popular cry here on the South Coast.

SUNDERLAND SUPPORTERS

The London and Southern England Branch of the Sunderland Supporters' Club has been in existence for 10 years. Already there is a membership of 430 many of whom follow their favourites all over England. A monthly newsletter is published by the Branch and party travel rates are available to all games.

Details of membership may be obtained by sending a stamped addressed envelope to Mr R. Clarke, 38 Valetta Road, Acton, London W3 7TN.

SEAGULL KITES ... BRIGHTON FESTIVAL

A Kite flying event is being held in conjunction with the Brighton Festival. It will take place at North Sheepcote Valley on Sunday, April 30. Competitions start at 10.30 a.m. and at 2.30 p.m., a special item is included with prizes for the best home-made kite to look like an ALBION SEAGULL.

Throughout the day there will be fun for all the family and enquiries about the event may be made to the Fringe Co-ordinator at 54 Old Steine, Brighton. (Tel: Brighton 29801, Ext 8104.) A stamped addressed envelope should be sent for a copy of the rules.

Report on the Slade appearance in another match programme.

13th: Rehearsing in Cannock.

16th: Don's diary: *"I was up at 10:00am. I got ready and drove to Heathrow to fly to Hamburg...... Drove to Kiel and the TV studio..... Did a rehearsal before coming back to the hotel."*

17th: Kiel - TV Show. Don's diary: *"Got up 10:30am, cleaned up and drove to the TV studio. A good day's work. We drove back to our hotel in Hamburg."*

18th: Slade fly back to the UK.
20th: Rehearsals, Cannock.
21st: Rehearsals cancelled for the day, as Jim wasn't feeling too well.
22nd: Rehearsals.
23rd: Press interviews with Nod and Don.

24th: Don's diary: *"I met everyone at the office so we could drive to Reading for a concert. GOOD ONE. Swinn took H and Jim back to Wolverhampton. Nod and myself came to London by Limo."*

Barn Records release the Slade single Give Us A Goal / Daddio. 2014121

Score with Slade

SLADE ARE looking for a high-scoring FA Cup quarter final at West Bromwich Albion on March 11, to promote their current single 'Give Us A Goal' (Barn 2014 121). Polydor has taken a goalmouth site at the ground for the match between WBA and league leaders Nottingham Forest. This is in addition to existing promotion on the single which includes music press advertising, space in the football magazine *Shoot*, giveaway whistles, song sheets and TV appearances by the band.

SLADE: 'Give Us A Goal' (Barn 2014 121). I'd like to see the oldies make it again, I really would. I always loved their gigs, just for the atmosphere. I think that's what they must have been thinking about when they wrote this song, because it recaptures the football fervour they used to build up. That's why it's a bit sad, because I don't think it's worked. I think they're groping in the dark (not a pleasant occupation when it's just for ideas), looking backwards for their future. The song's got plenty of guts, the typical rasping vocals, all that stuff, but it's missed the goal.

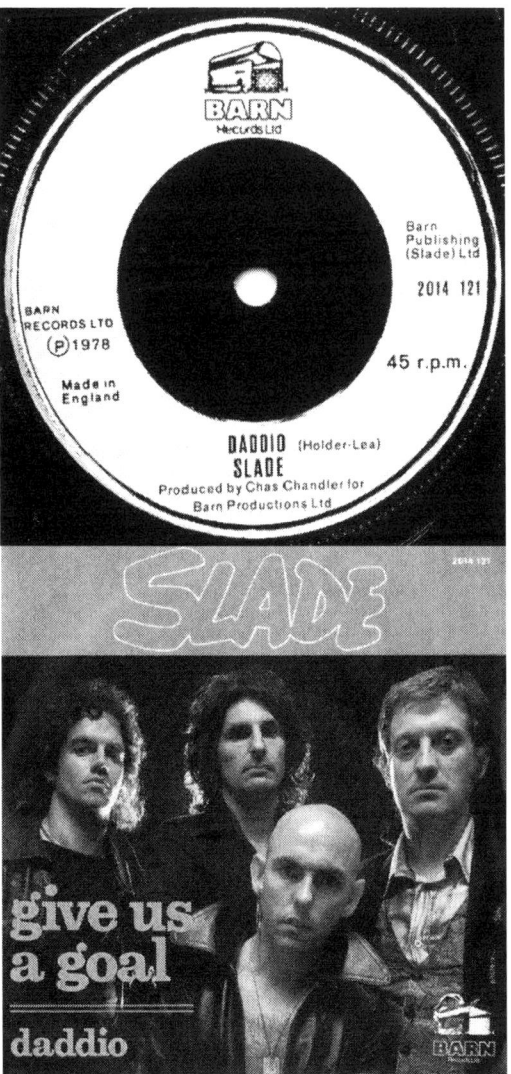

Cain's anal fixation

WITH REFERENCE to Barry Cain's review of the Dusty Springfield album, whilst agreeing with his comments on the record his generalisations over comebacks are quite ridiculous.

"Great comebacks have a habit of falling on their arses e.g. Slade." Does Mr Cain have an anal fixation? Slade certainly haven't fallen on their arses Their last single reached 32 with little promotion. Their album recieved unanimous critical acclaim. Their tour was a sell out.

Their new single 'Give Us A Goal' is brilliant and when it reaches the top perhaps Cain will keep his big gob shut. If he doesn't I'll get Noddy Holder to come around and make him suck one of Noddy's baby Charisse's dirty nappies.

Even Elvis Costello says 'Blame It On Cain'.

Ivor Bigun, Little Hampton.

● I think I love you Ivor. — B.C.

SLADE schießen ein To.

Auch die wiederauferstandenen Slade greifen wieder kräftig an – ihr mit Fußballstadion-Jubel untermaltes „Give us a

goal" (Barn Rec. 2041 121) bringt knappe drei Minuten lang handfesten Rock, der sich deutlich von ihren früheren Einfachst Fetzern unterscheidet. –

28th: Olympic Studios.
Slade re-recorded 'My Baby Left Me' and 'Give Us A Goal'.
These recordings were probably for TV backing track use.

MARCH 1978

3rd: Nod and Don caught the train to Newquay.

4th: Newquay, filming "Our Show".

6th: Chas Chandler, Nod and Don caught the train to Manchester. Nod and Don appeared at two radio stations that evening.

7th: Don's diary: *"I was up 07:00am, cleaned up and rehearsed and recorded the backing track and TV show (Get It Together). Muriel Young (TV producer) paid for a car to take Chas, Nod and myself back to London."*

Slade on Get It Together.
Dave used his unique John Birch Bat design guitar which was stolen shortly afterwards

8th: Olympic Studios. Don did some tom-tom overdubs on "Get On Up".

9th: Olympic studios going over 'Live-Recordings'.

10th: Olympic Studios overdubbing Tom-Toms and Hand claps.

14th: Cannock - rehearsals.

15th: Cannock - rehearsals.

16th: Cannock - rehearsals.

Tour dates announced. Slade were mainly playing clubs again, with the occasional large venue thrown in.

SLADE HIT THE ROAD

SLADE undertake one of their rare British tours, starting this weekend and running to mid-April. The tour, which aids promotion of their newly-released Barn single "Give Us A Goal", is an unusual mixture of major concerts, cabaret dates and back-to-the-roots club gigs — and it climaxes with a big London show at the Hammersmith Odeon.

Confirmed dates are Andover Country Bumpkin (tomorrow, Friday), Buckley Tivoli (Saturday), Birmingham Town Hall (March 21), Purley Tiffany's (22), Cromer West Runton Pavilion (23), Bury St Edmunds Focus Cinema (25), Sheffield Fiesta (26), Crawley Sports Centre (27), Wigan Casino (April 1), Bedford Nite Spot (2), London Southgate Royalty (4), Chesterfield Aquarius (5), Weston-super-Mare Webbington Country Club (6), Port Talbot Troubadour (7), Stroud Leisure Centre (8), Farnworth Blighty's (9), Bristol Colston Hall (10) and London Hammersmith Odeon (15)

SLADE AGAIN

WITH their new single 'Give Us A Goal' picking up radio plays, a revitalised Slade are back on the road in March. Their lengthy tour extends into April, when they end up with a major headlining date at London Hammersmith Odeon.

Full dates read: Andover Country Bumpkin March 17, Buckley Cheshire Tivoli 18, Birmingham Town Hall 21, Purley Tiffanys 22, West Runton Pavilion 23, Bury St Edmunds Focus Theatre 25, Sheffield Fiesta 26, Crawley Sports Centre 27, Wigan Casino April 1, Bedford Nite Spot 2, Southgate Royalty Ballroom 4, Chesterfield Aquarius 5, Weston - super - Mare Country Club 6, Port Talbot Troubador 7, Stroud Leisure Centre 8, Bolton Blightys 9, Bristol Colston Hall 10 and London Hammersmith Odeon 15.

SLADE CONCERT BARGAIN

POP CLUB members can obtain a 50p discount up to a maximum of two tickets for pop stars SLADE when they appear at the Royalty, Winchmore Hill, North London, next Tuesday.

The normal admission price is £2 but Pop Club members can have one ticket for £1·50 or two tickets for £3.

Just show your Pop Club membership cards at the door and see

Noddy Holder and Co. at a great discount.

SLADE, whose latest Give Us a Goal is out on the Barn label, hit the road this week for a tour mixing concert halls, cabaret venues and clubs. They have an Easter one-nighter at Sheffield Fiesta on Sunday, March 26 with Chesterfield's Aquarius to follow on April 5.

Back on the road for Slade

THERE'S a treat in store for Britain, and it starts tomorrow night at, of all places, the Country Bumpkin club in Andover, Hampshire ... Slade are going back on the road.

Having reached the very peak of fame in this country, and then seen new faces take the limelight and the glory, Slade have decided to return to what they do, and like doing, best — live performances.

So they have put the word out, and the bookings have come flowing in, though there's one glaring omission in the date sheet which I've been promised will be rectified — at the moment W'ton Civic Hall isn't on the list.

Said Slade's extrovert lead guitarist Dave Hill this week: "All our mates have been moaning about that, but it's just a case of there being no date available at the moment. We're going to fix one soon, but some of our W'ton fans are going to the one in Brum Town Hall next Tuesday."

Dave, chirpy as ever, seems glad, and even relieved to be back on the road with a new single, a Slade football anthem called Give Us A Goal, and a forthcoming live album to plug.

"What we decided to do was to get a bunch of dates to work with, and try to get to some of the places where they have never seen us before, and I think it will work to our advantage.

"We're working on a rock show; we just want to go and hit 'em between the eyes, there won't be any soft numbers. We experimented on records in the past, but when it came to doing the songs on stage the fire wasn't really there. Nod's voice is stronger than ever, and his voice demands the fire and thunder in the group's backing."

Slade still have a lot of fans, but by the time this tour is over I'm betting they will have many more once again.

John Ogden

Friday 17th - Country Bumpkin Club. Eastfield Road, Andover.
Don's diary and suitcase were stolen.

Saturday 18th – Tivoli Ballroom. Brunswick Road, Buckley, Flintshire
Support: Struggle

> **THIS FRIDAY, 10th MARCH**
> OVER 25's CABARET DANCE
> With sensational rock n roll act
> **FREDDIE AND THE FINGERS!!!**
> Dancing to the **DOOLEY BAND**
> 8 p.m. 'till 1 a.m. Admission £1. No casual dress
>
> Saturday, 11th March
> **BEAT NIGHT with**
> **FLYING MACHINE**
> *PLUS DISCO*
> 8 p.m. till 1 p.m. Admission before 9.30 p.m.
> 80p after £1
>
> ---
> **FORTHCOMING ATTRACTION**
> Saturday, 18th March
> **SLADE**
> **STRUGGLES**

Tuesday 21st - Town Hall. Victoria Square, Birmingham.
Support: Struggle

Andrew Page Entertainments presents

SLADE
+ STRUGGLE
**BIRMINGHAM TOWN HALL,
TUESDAY 21st MARCH
BRISTOL COLSTON HALL,
MONDAY 10th APRIL**

Tickets £1.50, £2.00 & £2.50 obtainable from Birmingham Town Hall Box Office
tel: 021 236 2392
Bristol Colston Hall Box Office tel: 0272 22957

It's back to the beginning again for Slade

by ROBERT MOORE

A COME-BACK campaign by Slade, once one of the Midlands' most famous pop groups, begins at Birmingham Town Hall tonight — but only 60 per cent of the tickets have been sold.

"Far from being has-beens, we now feel revitalised and ready to get back in to the big time," said lead singer Noddy Holder (left) today.

"Some friends in Birmingham keep an eye on it for me and keep the gardens tidy," said Noddy.

"I don't know what I want to do with it. It's difficult to settle down in my business. But it is a good investment and will never lose value."

Slade have struggled to regain their former popularity after a two-year absence on a United States tour.

He was in his native Walsall — the other three members of the group are from the Black Country — preparing for their first concert in Birmingham for eight months.

The tickets already sold means that the Town Hall will probably be full — but in their heyday a Slade show would have been a box office "blockbuster."

Their recent record "My Baby Left Me" reached position 31 in the charts but they have high hopes for a newly released single, "Give Us a Goal".

Mean time they are on a long concert tour, a tour which includes such "second division" venues as Taunton, Wigan and Bury St. Edmunds.

Noddy is not living in the luxury bungalow in Ladywood Road, Four Oaks, which he bought for nearly £50,000 some years ago.

The bungalow, previously owned by Mr. Alan Maudsley, the former Birmingham City Architect jailed for corruption offences, stands empty.

SLADE RELIGHT THE OLD FLAME

Well, Slade are back, and the fans are just as crazee as ever!

Tuesday's concert at Birmingham Town Hall proved that neither the group nor their fans have lost enthusiasm or energy.

No sooner had the band stepped on the stage than the place was in uproar. All seating plans and ticket allocations were whipped aside as a mass of youngsters rushed to the front of the stage. And Slade tore into them with the fire and thunder of old, their long years together as a band telling strongly in the way they powered into the music.

The only changes are in their appearance. They're not so flashily dressed any more, and Dave now has his famous shaven head. But the music and the atmosphere are just the same; non-stop rock and non-stop fun.

After starting with the timeless favourite Hear Me Calling, they did a complete programme of their own material – their old hits, rockers from the later albums, a song or two from their film Flame. And it was great to hear. Beneath all the roar and bombast there are some subtle chordings and counterpoints going on, particularly from Jimmy Lea's bass, and listening to the concert after a break of some time brings it home just how good a writing team are Jim and Noddy Holder.

It was a great night for the band and for the audience who cheered, waved and stamped on request and sang beautifully in time and in tune. It can't be a coincidence that Slade audiences always seem more alive and responsive to what's going on than practically any other rock crowd I've seen.

John Ogden
Wolverhampton express & Star

Wednesday 22nd - Tiffanys Nightclub. Brighton Road, Purley

Slade cum bak

SLADE have started their first tour in over a year, which coincides with the release of their new single, 'Give Us A Goal'.

They have dates lined up at West Runton Pavilion March 23, St Ives Recreation Centre 25, Sheffield Fiesta 26, Crawley Sports Centre 27, Wigan Casino April 1, Bedford Nite Spot 2, Southgate Royalty Ballroom 4, Chesterfield Aquarius 5, Weston Super Mare Country Club 6, Port Talbot Troubadour 7, Stroud Leisure Centre 8, Bolton Blighties 9, Bristol Colston Hall 10, London Hammersmith Odeon 15.

Thursday 23rd - West Runton Pavilion
Support: Eazie

Friday 24th - Reading University Rag Ball
Support: Kevin Coyne / Brian Parrish Band

Saturday 25th - Focus Cinema. Brentgovel Street. Bury St Edmunds.

Sunday 26th - Fiesta Club. Norton Road, Sheffield

Monday 27th - Sports Centre, Crawley
Support: Struggle

CRAWLEY'S ROCK'N'ROLL FANS ARE SLAYED BY SLADE

For those who bothered to turn up to see Slade at the Sports Centre on Easter Monday, it was a magical night. The group, once the idols of thousands, treated their audience to rock 'n' roll music at its very best, storming through such hits as Get Down And Get With It and Gudbuy T' Jane.

But it was not only the excellence of the band's performance which was the focal point of the evening, but also the amazing apathy shown by the rock fans of Crawley in failing to support the gig.

This must raise a question mark over the Sports Centre as a venue for rock music. Do the young people of Crawley really care about places to go and things to see in their town?

On the evidence of the 400 or so present on Monday, they have obviously not yet made up their minds.

Disappointed promoter Nick Wilson, the man who must shoulder the huge losses, said: "I take small consolation in the fact that I, and the rest of the audience, witnessed the greatest rock show this town has ever seen."

It was difficult to disagree with Noddy Holder, the band's powerful singer, when he said that although the crowd was the smallest the band had played to on their current tour, he had enjoyed himself and they would be glad to return at a later date.

The spectacular lighting and excellent sound system implemented the group's musical expertise - this was indeed a concert the like of which Crawley is unlikely to see again. The venue was perfect, Mr Wilson's organisation faultless, and the music first class. The question is not do the kids in Crawley want a place such as the Sports Centre - but do they deserve one?

Steve Gillham
Crawley Observer

**AT LAST!
IN CRAWLEY!**

The Rock Concert you cannot afford to miss!

Easter Monday, March 27, 7.30pm

SLADE

at Crawley Sportcentre

+ STRUGGLE plus KELLYS ROAD SHOW

Tickets in advance £1.60, on the door £1.80

Saturday, April 29: MOTORS + SUPPORT

Tuesday 28th - Lintig, Germany

Cum off it

I AM very fed up with the disinterest shown by the press to that fabulous group Slade. They offer the best brand of rock music in the country and they outclass Rush, Rainbow and Quo, all of whom I've seen. — **M. Bundy.**

The fans were still sticking up for the band.

APRIL 1978

Saturday 1st – Wigan Casino. Station Road, Wigan

```
WIGAN
CASINO CLUB
STATION ROAD, WIGAN              TEL. 43501
FRIDAY —                    (7 30 pm to 11 45 pm)
         SOUL NIGHT
            with Russ Winstanley
      Admission 45p           Members Only
SATURDAY —                    (7 30 to 11 45 pm)
         SPECIAL ATTRACTION!!
             The Fabulous
            SLADE
         PLUS DJ PAUL McCRACKEN
              Admission £2.00
SATURDAY/SUNDAY MORNING   (12 30 to 10 am)
      Soul Club allnighter
      Admission £1.50          Members Only
WEDNESDAY —                   (7.30 to 11 30)
         SOUL NIGHT
            with Russ Winstanley
              Admission 30p
```

Hear Me Calling / Get on up / Be / Take me bak 'ome / Burning in the heat of love / Everyday / Far far away / Them kinda monkeys can't swing / bass / violin solos / Gudbuy T'Jane / Dave's solo / My baby left me / Give us a goal / Mama weer all crazee now. Encores: Get down and get with it / One eyed Jacks with moustaches / Cum on feel the noize / Keep on rockin'

On the early 1978 tour dates, Dave persevered with the shaven-headed look and a head-to-toe leather outfit, which meant he sweated some weight off every night on stage. Jim went for a leather jacket and white jeans and shirt. Nod wore a tartan jacket. Don was usually stripped to the waist after a few songs.

Sunday 2nd - Regal Cinema. Station Road, Ashington.

```
CITY HALL, NEWCASTLE. Tues. April 11th at 7.30 p.m.
Quarry Promotions presents
RORY GALLAGHER
AND HIS BAND in Concert
Tickets: £3, £2.50 and £2 from CITY HALL
BOX OFFICE (Tel. 20007). Open 10.30-5.30 p.m. daily
```

```
Sunday at the REGAL
Regal Cinema, Station Road, Ashington
In Concert
SLADE
Plus support
Sunday, April 2, at 7.30 p.m.
Tickets £2.50, £2, £1.50
Available from Music Boxes, Blyth and Bedlington
and Wallaw Cinema, Ashington
Or Tel. Ashington 812231, 9 a.m.-9 p.m.
```

```
CITY HALL, NEWCASTLE. Friday, April 14th, at 7.30 p.m.
Kennedy Street Enterprises Limited present:
The Unique sounds of the world's leading electronic organist
KLAUS WUNDERLICH
IN CONCERT + special guests SWEET SUBSTITUTE
Tickets. £2.50, £2, £1.50 & £1 available from:
CITY HALL BOX OFFICE Tel. 20007 Open 10.30-5.30 daily
```

```
CITY HALL, NEWCASTLE. Mon., May 15, at 8 p.m.
Derek Block presents
DON McLEAN
IN CONCERT
Tickets: £3, £2.50, £2 and £1.50 from CITY HALL
BOX OFFICE (Tel. 20007) Daily 10.30-5.30 p.m.
```

Tuesday 4th - Royalty. Winchmore Hill Rd, Southgate, London
Support: Struggle

LONDON'S MOST POPULAR NITE SPOT
Winchmore Hill Road, Southgate N14
(opposite Southgate Underground — Picc Line)
01-886 4112

Thurs., 30th:	**CRAZY CAVAN**
Fri., 31st:	**MUNGO JERRY**
Sat., 1st:	**IMPERIALS**
Tues., 4th:	**SLADE**

Tickets on sale now
20th April: **CARL PERKINS** and **BO DIDDLEY**
13th May: **BRASS CONSTRUCTION**

Wednesday 5th - Leas Cliffs Hall. The Leas, Folkestone
Don's diary: *"I was up at 08:30, cleaned up. Nod and myself had breakfast together, before doing an interview on TV...??????. Afterwards, we drove back to London to catch up with H & Jim.*

We all drove to Folkestone. Did our sound check. Had a so-so show... Drove back to London, stopping for 'fish n chips' on the way. H & Swinn stayed at my place."

April 6th:
Thursday 6th - Country Club. Webbington Rd, Weston Super-Mare.
Don's diary: *"Left to play the Webbington Country Club. Another so-so show. One of the guys from Four Steps Beyond (the group we played with in Dortmund in 1965) was at the show. Drove back to Wolverhampton"*

SLADE: ANOTHER EIGHT

SLADE have added another eight dates to their current tour — at Aberystwyth University (April 18), Edinburgh University (21), Glasgow University (22), Wolverhampton Civic Hall (24), Coventry Theatre (27), Hull College of Education (28), Plymouth Polytechnic (29) and Portsmouth Guildhall (30). But their previously-reported gig at Port Talbot Troubadour tomorrow (Friday) is cancelled.

Friday 7th - Troubador Club - Port Talbot (Cancelled)

Saturday 8th - Leisure Centre. Stretford Road, Stroud.
Don's diary: *"Drove to Stroud - had a fair show. Nod, Swinn and myself drove back to Wolverhampton (The Happy Car). Went for a curry when we got there."*

Sunday 9th –Blighty's. Chapel St, Farnworth, Bolton.
Support: Paper Plane

Hear Me Calling / Get on up / Be / Take me bak 'ome / My baby left me / Burning in the heat of love / Everyday / Far far away / Them kinda monkeys can't swing / bass / violin solos / Gudbuy T'Jane / Give us a goal / Mama weer all crazee now. Encores: Get down and get with it / One eyed Jacks with moustaches / Cum on feel the noize

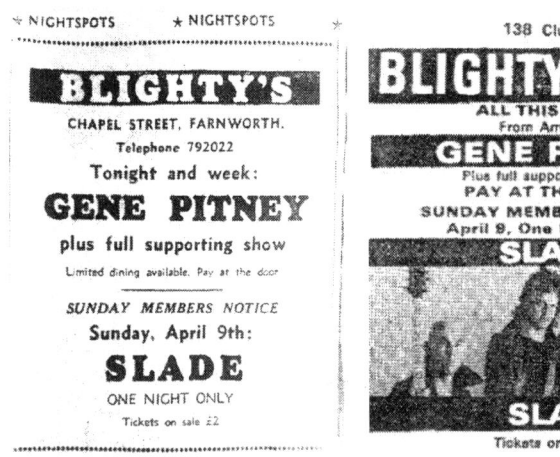

Don's diary: "Drove to Bolton. Had a good show. We all drove home together, but Nod, Swinn and myself went to the curry-house again."

According to local press, the location is now apparently an old folks home.

Monday 10th - Colston Hall. Colston Street. Bristol

Tuesday 11th
Aquarius Club. Sheffield Rd,
Chesterfield, Derbyshire.

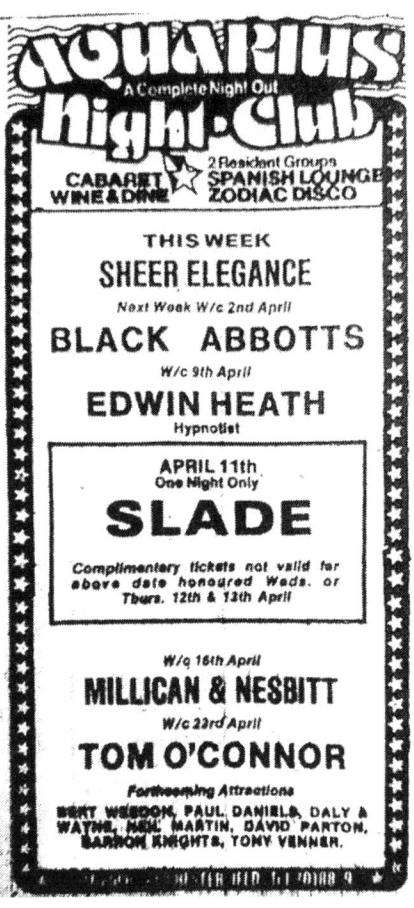

Wednesday 12th
Empire Theatre. High St West,
Sunderland
Support: Geordie

Slade
Bristol

NEVER MIND the quality, feel the noise, eh? True to form, Slade are killingly loud. the house isn't full either, but those that are here are fanatical and also surprisingly young. It seems that Slade maintain an uncanny rapport with the 12 to 15 age bracket which doesn't seem to wilt despite the fact that their original early Seventies fans must have grown up and moved on.

Personally, I've never paid much attention to 'em. They're a fair to good heavy rock band with a talent for hit singles and catchy tunes that depend on pretty standard rock clichés and what really elevates them is the quality of Noddy Holder's voice and the simple, good feeling that they bring to the music.

They know their audience and their audience knows them — total empathy, no pretensions about the art of their music, a dirty good time is what they're after and is exactly what they achieve. These kids simply want to punch the air in time to the music and just feel good, feel part of something. This is really a football crowd with a band instead of a team, but there's no violence 'cos they're all on the same side.

Now, the fact that I don't care much for playing 'Simon says' call and response games all night ("Are ya all right?" — "Yeah, we're all right") to average mainstream rock doesn't really matter. What matters is the feeling the audience gets of release and togetherness which Slade are masters at providing for them.

RAB

Don's diary: *"I was up at 12:30, cleaned up and drove to Sunderland. GOOD gig - the band Geordie were on with us. Their singer, Brian Johnson, now sings with AC/DC. GOOD show. Drove to London afterwards."*

Rock fans wreak havoc in Empire

SEATS and brass rails were smashed and twisted at the Sunderland Empire last night, as rock group Slade worked a young audience to fever pitch.

House manager, Mr Ron Jameson said today that the cost of the damage had not been counted, but it was expected to run to hundreds of pounds.

"The youngsters tend to stand on the arms and backs of the seats which smashes the framework, and the sheer weight of numbers pressing up against the brass rails bent them easily."

He added that although there was an audience of only 800 — less than half the theatre's capacity — they had been very involved in the performance, and at times some became carried away with the highly charged atmosphere.

SIMILAR ACTS

"It is something we have begun to expect when this kind of group plays here," said Mr Jameson. "We usually have commercial men acting between ourselves and the group to take care of this kind of thing. I do not know who will be responsible for the insurance this time but the theatre will be covered."

However the incident has not discouraged Empire management from booking similar acts. Said Mr Jameson: "Our aim is to be the people's theatre and cater for all kinds of interests. We try to provide entertainment right across the board, and we will be happy to continue with this kind of concert."

Already lined up for future dates are Showaddywaddy and Osibisa.

Slade — their fans caused damaged at the Empire last night estimated at hundreds of pounds.

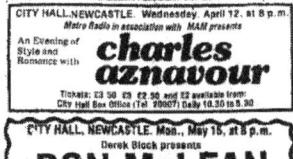

CITY HALL, NEWCASTLE. Wednesday, April 12, at 8 p.m.
Metro Radio in association with MAM presents
An Evening of Style and Romance with
charles aznavour
Tickets: £3.50, £3, £2.50, £2 and £2 available from: City Hall Box Office (Tel. 20007) Daily 10.30 to 5.30

CITY HALL, NEWCASTLE. Mon., May 15, at 8 p.m.
Derek Block presents
DON McLEAN
IN CONCERT
Tickets: £3, £2.50, £2 and £1.50 from CITY HALL BOX OFFICE (Tel. 20007). Daily 10.30 to 5.30 p.m.

EMPIRE THEATRE SUNDERLAND
Wednesday, April 12, at 8.45 p.m.
SLADE in CONCERT
plus "GEORDIE"
Tickets in advance at Box Office
£1, £2, £3

CITY HALL, NEWCASTLE. Thursday, April, 13th, at 8 p.m.
Mervyn Conn presents
The Original Rock 'n Roll Show. Featuring
CARL PERKINS
BO DIDDLEY & MATCHBOX
Tickets £3, £2.50 & £1.50 from CITY HALL BOX OFFICE (Tel. 20007). Daily 10.30 to 5.30 p.m.

CITY HALL, NEWCASTLE. Friday, April 14th, at 7.30 p.m.
Kennedy Street Enterprises Limited presents
The Unique sounds of the world's leading electronic organist
KLAUS WUNDERLICH
IN CONCERT + special guests SWEET SUBSTITUTE
Tickets £2.50, £2, £1.50 & £1 available from: CITY HALL BOX OFFICE Tel. 20007 Open 10.30-5.30

Nod and Jim in harmony in Sunderland.

Thursday April 13th:
Venue unknown.
Don's diary: *"Had a good show...??????"*

Friday April 14th 1978:
Olympic Studio to record the backing track for 'Cheggers Plays Pop'.

Saturday 15th
Odeon.
Queen Caroline Street, Hammersmith, London

Don's diary: *"I was up at 11:00am, cleaned up and drove to Hammersmith Odeon. Did the sound check and had a good show. We all had a drink in the 'artistes' bar before driving back to Wolverhampton."*

Hammersmith Odeon

SLADE

THEY say the tempo of life is speeding up. And so it is, as Slade demonstrated at the Hammersmith Odeon on Saturday night. The good old days are now only half a decade in the past — the nostalgia gap gets smaller all the time.

Though by no means a packed house, the Odeon audience was at one with Noddy and the lads — and this was both good and bad. It was good because Slade needed a welcome. It was bad because some of the audience were too fanatical to give the support band, the Brakes, an even break. The Brakes are sort of middle-of-the-wave, and they put down a tight, good-humoured set, the best number of which was their last, "Bits And Pieces." The energy they displayed on stage just goes to show how things have changed since Slade were riding high — Slade, the great high energy band of their time, came across almost lethargic by comparison.

Between announcements concerning their happiness (and relief?) to be back at 'Ammersmif ,and after quite a lot of "Take Me Bak Home," "Goodbye T'Jane," "Get Down And Get With It," and "We're All Crazee Now," Slade reeled off their new anthem, "Give Us A Goal," which will be of considerable interest to rabid footy fans and of no interest to anyone else. Perhaps there is some fundamental comment on our times in the spectacle of an audience scrabbling for rolls of toilet paper during a rock concert.

It seems we English take a perverse delight in wasting our best rock singers — Roger Chapman springs to mind, and now Noddy Holder. Shaved heads and electric violin solos do not great music make, and it is a shame that a singer of Holder's talent, originality, and force is bogged down in such a mire of sound and fury. I guess that's show biz.

One last word: praise to the staff of the Odeon, who battled to keep order with a minimum of hassle and a maximum of tolerant discretion. Well done, you courageous few. — DAVID BLAKE.

GUDBUY TO PAIN

SLADE, Hammersmith Odeon, London.

BACK in the days when I was but a wee weeny-bopper, Slade were my idols. Never mind The Osmonds; Slade, Bowie, Bolan, they were my heritage at a time when I thought New York Dolls were Tiny Tears' colonial cousins. If six years ago I had been offered a couple of tickets to a Slade gig, I would have thought myself the bee's knees.

When the situation arose a few days ago, I was less ecstatic. Skeletons were dragged from the cupboard and my credibility blown sky-high. Tastes change, people ch nge, but Slade don't.

Well Dave Hill has swopped the silver glitter for leather trews and a Kojak cut, and Noddy sports similar lower garments, a frilly shirt and impressive paunch; but underneath they're still the proverbial working class heroes.

The audience was 95 per cent male teenagers who clapped, cheered, sang and swayed to all the old favourites. 'Gudbuy T'Jane', 'Take Me Bak 'Ome', 'Far Far Away', 'Mama We're All Crazy Now' . . . the list continues, as Noddy introduces almost every song with 'Now an oldie, remember . . .'

Those numbers not culled from the singles catalogue each had a trick or treat to ensure a firm imprint upon the memory. Dry ice and rainbow lighting for 'Burning In A Sea Of Love', or drum, bass and (lengthy) violin solos from Don Powell and Jimmy Lea. They haven't forgotten the tricks of the trade.

They first start a rousing chorus of 'You'll Never Walk Alone' before launching into their new single, 'Give Us A Goal'; amidst the cascading toilet rolls, the atmosphere is closer to a football match than a major concert.

Holder's voice is stronger than ever, with a quality of coarse grit, but the strength of an ox. Musically, other than Lea, the band are little more than competent. Their main strength is their rhythms, which form a pounding basis for their simple, but effective melodies. Even on the only ballad of the evening, 'Everyday', the swaying of the crowd was as spontaneous as the foot-stomping to 'Get Down And Get With It', the encore.

The surprise, for me, of the evening was that the showman proved to be the seemingly quiet Lea, who continually leapt from the speakers, ran along the catwalks and invaded Hill's less active region of the stage. He even set out to deafen himself by first placing his head in the bass bin, and then the drum, yet still escaped with his head soldered to his shoulders.

I'm not sure I was glad to be taken back, but although Slade are no longer rising stars, they can still pack a punch with their greatest hits . . . live. **KELLY PIKE**

MEL BUSH PRESENTS

SLADE

PLUS SUPPORT

Saturday, April 15
HAMMERSMITH ODEON, 8 p.m.

Tickets: £2.50, £2.00, £1.50
Available Box Office. Tel. 01-748 4081

16th: Travel to Manchester - TV show. Showaddywaddy also featured.

17th: Olympic Studios.

Tuesday 18th – University, Aberystwyth
Support: The Depressions.
Don's diary: *"I was up at 09:15am, cleaned up. Arranged with Rose-Morris (the Ludwig distributors in UK) to get some percussion stuff for the studio. Nod picked me up to drive to Wolverhampton. From there we all drove to Aberystwyth. Did a so-so gig with Chas's new signings The Depressions. I drove back to London with our Lighting crew."*

Wednesday 19th: Don's diary: *"I got up at 12:30 and called Jim Wilmore at Rose-Morris. Met him at the factory and we sorted out some percussion stuff for me. Jim called for me to have a listen to the drumming on the Beatles "Strawberry Fields Forever" to use on one of his new songs 'I'm Mad'."*

20th: Don's diary: *"Spent all day in Advision going over 'I'm Mad'. In the end we went back to what we had already recorded. IT WAS ALREADY THERE."*

Friday 21st - University, Edinburgh

Saturday 22nd - University, Glasgow
Don's diary: *"Stayed in bed until 12:30, when H came round to borrow some shaving foam. Had a so-so show. We drove back to Wolverhampton afterwards. Dad was getting ready for work when I got home."*

Close shave for Slade crew

SLADE'S seven-man road crew are counting themselves lucky to be appearing at the band's home town concert at Wolverhampton Civic Hall, on Monday.

They have only just got over the fright of crashing in their Mercedes van while travelling down the M6 at speed.

The lads, most of them from the West Midlands, were very lucky, because the puncture which caused the accident happened when they were passing over a bridge. They said it was only because they hit the parapet that they didn't roll over completely.

The van was badly damaged. I hear both axles were shorn off by the impact.

□ □ □

POP GROUP manager Malcolm West, who has steered three groups to win on New Faces over the years, is opening a new nightclub in the town this week.

Called Mary's Moustache, it's in Castle Street, and it's planned to be a disco combined with night club, wine bar and restaurant.

Monday 24th
Civic Hall.
North Street,
Wolverhampton

Don's diary:
"I got up at 12:30. Cleaned up to play the Civic Hall.... Good show. Drank at the Trumpet before going on to Olivers for late drinks."

Hear Me Calling / Get on up / Be / Take me bak 'ome / My baby left me / Burning in the heat of love / Everyday / Far far away / Them kinda monkeys can't swing / bass / violin solos / Gudbuy T'Jane / Give us a goal / Mama weer all crazee now.
Encores: Get down and get with it / One eyed Jacks with moustaches / Cum on feel the noize / Keep on rockin'

Tuesday 25th - Theatre Royal. Claskgate, Lincoln

Wednesday 26th - Theatre Royal. Claskgate, Lincoln
Don's diary: *"Cleaned up and played Lincoln again. During the afternoon we all went to see "Close Encounters Of The Third Kind". I remember*

when the aliens came off their space ship, I shouted: "Dave Hill". WE ALL CRACKED UP. Had a good show, Swinn and myself drove back to Wolverhampton, having a drink at The Lafayette and Olivers."

Thursday 27th – Coventry Theatre.

COVENTRY THEATRE

Box Office open from 10 a.m. ☎ Coventry 23141/2

MAY 15-20 Evgs. 7.30. Mat. Sat. 2.30 LONDON FESTIVAL BALLET	Mon., Tues., Wed. Romeo & Juliet Thurs., Fri., Sat., Giselle, Conservatoire
SAT., APRIL 22, 7.30 RORY GALLAGHER & HIS BAND	FRI., MAY 12, 7.30 ELKIE BROOKS
THURS., APRIL 27, 7.30 SLADE	SAT., MAY 13, 6 & 8.30 CHARLIE PRIDE
WED., MAY 10, 8.00 THE TUBES	SUN., MAY 21, 7.30 GEORGE BENSON
SUN., MAY 28, 7.30 IAN DURY	

Friday 28th - Hull College of Further Education.

Saturday 29th - Polytechnic. Portsmouth
Don's diary: *"Drove to Plymouth for a good show. I drove home with the lighting crew."*

Sunday 30th - Guild Hall. Guildhall Street, Portsmouth
Don's diary: *"I got home 07:30. Went straight to bed. Found out my, American Express card had been used by someone."*

MAY 1978

Thursday 4th - Behan's Club – Jersey
Don's diary: *"We all met at the office (Upper Montague St, W1) to drive to Gatwick. Met Chas. We all flew to Jersey. Had a good show. At the hotel we were staying in Pete Abberley and Johnnie O'Hara (who used to be in the Californians from Wolverhampton) were performing a 'duo' set in the hotel bar."*

Friday 5th - Behan's Club – Jersey
Saturday 6th - Behan's Club – Jersey

Behans was formerly the West Park Pavilion. It closed in 1980.

9th:
Don's diary: "The Police called from Andover to say they had my stolen suitcase from the start of the tour."

10th:
Don's diary: "Spent all day in the studio recording "Ruby Red" again. Mick Legg, JJ, Swinn and H stayed at my place."

11th:
Don's diary: "Spent all day at Bronze Studios recording "Ruby Red" again. 'Messed' around with the Advision tapes."

Friday 12th - Polytechnic – Newcastle
Don's diary: *"American Express called about my stolen card. Met Nod at Kings Cross Station to travel to Newcastle Upon Tyne. Jim and H were late.. Good show, I drove back to Wolverhampton. Dad was just going to work when I arrived."*

16th:
Don's diary: *"I drove to Andover to collect my stolen suitcase. Diners Club and American Express let me know that I wasn't responsible for the monies spent on my stolen cards. I collected my suitcase with all my belongings intact. I then took the two CID officers for dinner. They then gave me a Police escort to the outskirts of Andover."*

17th: Spent all day in the studio recording "It's All Right Buy Me"

Saturday 18th - Nutz Club. Newton Road, Swansea.

Friday 19th - Aston University, Birmingham

20th Glasgow University:
Don's diary: "Swinn picked me up to drive to Glasgow.. So-so show. Drove back to Wolverhampton after the show."

Sunday 21st - Variety Club – Batley, Yorkshire.

22nd: Don's diary:
"We had a delayed / late rehearsals as Charlie (sound engineer) had taken the equipment lock up keys to New York with him. Eventually rehearsed. I went with Swinn to Stafford to see The Depressions."

Tuesday 23rd
Lafayette Club. Thornley Street, Wolverhampton
Rehearsals

Wednesday 24th
Ruffles Club. Diamond St, Aberdeen, Scotland

LIVE ON STAGE

ONE PERFORMANCE ONLY

WED. 24th MAY

Doors open 8pm

Admission : £4 - £3 - £2

Diamond Street   Tel. 29092/3

Friday 26th
Coatham Bowl, Redcar

Saturday 27th
Norbreck Castle Hotel.
Norcalympia Hall
Queens Promenade,
Blackpool
Support: Strife

Don's diary: "Drove to Blackpool. No sound check, as our equipment truck was having problems with the brakes. Good show. Drove home after."

NORBRECK CASTLE HOTEL
NORCALYMPIA
QUEENS PROMENADE, BLACKPOOL

Bank Holiday Saturday, May 27th

SLADE
Plus STRIFE

D.J. Mark Simpson

8 pm — 1 am   Bar   Snacks etc

Admission £1.50 advance or £2.00 on night.

Bank Holiday Monday, May 29th

10 HOUR EXTRAVAGANZA
3 pm — 1 am

STEEL PULSE
SUPERCHARGE
JAB JAB — VARDIS — MAGIC
D.J. Mark Simpson

Advance tickets £1.50 or £2.00 on day.

Advance tickets on sale at the Norbreck Castle or by post, enclosing PO and SAE to Denis Johnson, Norbreck Castle Hotel, Queens Promenade, Blackpool. Eng. Phone Blackpool 52341.

SOUTH BANK POLYTECHNIC S.U. Rotary Street, S.E.1
Tel 01-261 1525
Friday May 12th at 8 pm

Re-raunch for Slade

WITV skin 'eads back in the news and every sort of rock music there's ever been enjoying some kind of revival it was only a matter of time before Slade cropped up again.

Not that they are skinheads any more but their original publicity launch had them as the country's first such band playing a much raunchier form of music than is associated with that particular fashion today.

In those days the Midland band who came together in a Wolverhampton coffee bar when vocalist Neville (Noddy) Holder was bemoaning the demise of his former band the Mavericks and the three other members had just lost their vocalist from the In Betweens, their music was loud and raw.

Their skinhead look was soon dropped (except for Dave Hill who shaved all his hair off and has only recently bothered rowing it again) when the adverse publicity surrounding that movement and the music they were playing worked against them.

They met up with ex-Animals member Chas Chandler who abbreviated their Ambrose Slade label to its familiar shorter form, encouraged them to write their own numbers and saw them hit the charts for the first time with "Get Down And Get With It."

Slademania had begun and from "Coz I Luv You" in October 1971 through to "Nobody's Fool" in March 1976 the band were rarely out of the charts.

In many respects they pre-dated punk banners and football scarves, boots and braces were the order of the day for a Slade concert—yet it was that musical revolution which knocked them from their pedestal.

But they are still a working band and the line-up has remained unchanged over the years. New material is on its way and together with their old favourites it can be heard at the band's Norbreck Castle Night Spot booking on Wednesday.

Speak up, I've just heard Slade

THE latest rock survivors to wash up on the shores of Blackpool last night probably wondered why anyone ever reported them missing.

After a "quiet" period of four years Slade blasted their way back into the consciousness of the converted and the curious at the Norbreck Nite Spot. Anyone on the streets of Blackburn probably also got an earful.

"Come On Feel the Noise" — one of their selection of anthems — took on a new meaning as the tons of equipment normally reserved for concert halls swamped the Norbreck stage — and provided a sound blanket that everyone seemed to want to share.

With the added lighting paraphernalia it added up to an experience the audience will talk about for months . . . just as soon as their hearing returns.

While Slade's set included many of their hit singles, among them "Get Down and Get With It" and "Goodbye to Jane" — the rest of the night was a rock anthology borrowing from Hendrix, Bolan, Steppenwolf and others with selections from the band's new "Six of the Best" EP. "It's Alright When I'm Dancing," aimed at the charts, was delivered with the same aggression that was their hallmark in the early 70s, and should see them firmly re-established in the early 80s.

DAVID UPTON

Sunday 28th - Willows Club, Weaste Lane, Salford.
Don's diary: "Drove to Manchester for the last show. Great gig."

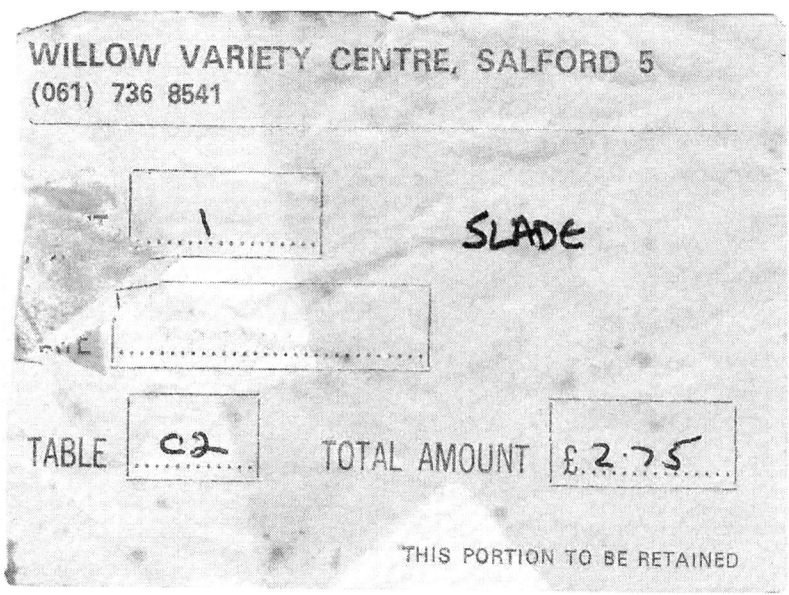

The Willows closed down in 2012.

Tuesday 30th - Advision Studio
Recorded "It's Alright Buy Me"

Wednesday 31st:
Advision Studio.

JUNE 1978

June 1st: Spent all day at, Advision recording.

June 2nd: Spent the last day at Advision.

June 3rd: Olympic Studios, going over the 'live' recordings.

June 4th: Olympic Studios, going over the 'live' recordings.

June 7th: Don's diary: *"I called H as he and Jim had been to see ELO in Stafford. Not impressed...."*

June 10th: Don's diary: *"Swinn and Mickey Legg arrived from Wolverhampton. Nod and Leandra also met us at my place. Made our way to Wembley Arena to see ELO. Met everyone backstage and drunk most of their booze. Methinks they were miming partly to backing tapes."*

June 13th: Don's diary: "The CID called from Brighton to arrange a court case to do with my stolen suitcase. They needed to know when I would be free. I gave them my schedule. John (singer with Sparrow) called. He wanted to fix an appointment with Mike Hayles (Chas's label manager at Barn)."

June 14th: Don's diary: *Nod called about coming round for a chat. My old school, Etheridge Secondary School made contact with me about giving a lecture there. Spent the night at the Sparrow gig."*

June 15th: Don's diary: *"All of us had a meeting with Chas. It was agreed that we would now produce our own records. He would produce one more. Went with Mike Hayles to see ELO again at Wembley."*

June 20th: Spent all day in Olympic going over the 'live' stuff.

June 21st 1978: Spent all day in Olympic. Don later went to another studio to work with Tommy Boyce (The Monkees' writer and producer).

June 22nd: Andover CID called to say the thieves who stole Don's suit case, had been fined £200.

June 26th: Rehearsals at the Lafayette in Wolverhampton.

June 27th: Rehearsals at the Lafayette in Wolverhampton.

June 28th: Spent all day in the studio, recording "I've Been Rejected".

June 29th: All day in the studio finishing "I've Been Rejected". This song was later retitled Rock And Roll Bolero.

June 30th: Don played Sparrow's recordings to Mike Hayles to no avail.

JULY 1978

July 1st: Don went to see David Bowie at Earl's Court.
July 3rd: Spent all day in the studio.

July 4th: Don's diary: *"Spent all day in the studio recording Rock n' Roll Bolero again."*

July 5th: Don's diary: *"Spent all day and all night going over "Rock n' Roll Bolero"*

July 7th: Olympic Studios going over the 'live' recordings.
July 9th: Olympic Studio.

July 10th: Gered Mankowitz's studio for a photo session. Evening IBC Studio.
July 11th: Mixing session in IBC studio.

July 12th: Wolverhampton - rehearsals.
July 13th: Cannock - Rehearsals.

July 20th: Slade flew to Copenhagen. Then on to Aalborg for show. Don's diary: *"Not a very good show....."*

July 21st: Tvedhallen - Tved, Denmark
Don's diary: *"Drove to Skagen. Jim had to get his back fixed????? Better show than last night..."*

July 22nd: Don's diary: *"Show in Denmark?"*

July 23rd: Køge Byfest (Køge Civic Festival)
Don's diary: *"Flew to Warsaw, Poland. Promoter George met us. Checked in the hotel. Ate and drank there all night..."*

July 24th: Sopot – Poland
Don's diary: *"I was still in bed when JJ called. Everyone was in the lobby waiting for me. We flew to Sopot. H and myself sat in the sun all afternoon? Did sound check. Good show. Early one. Back to the hotel to eat and drink"*

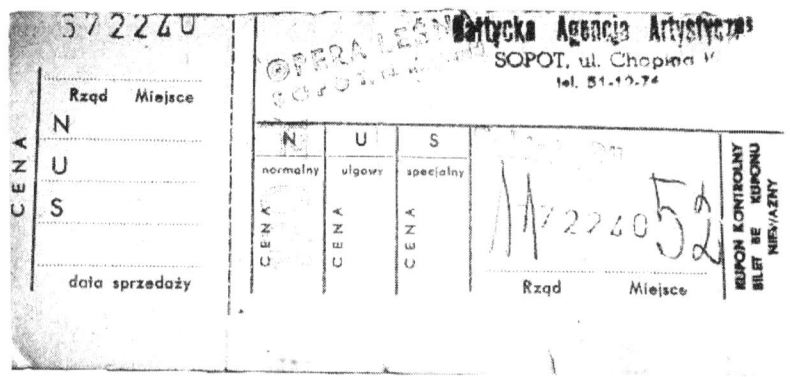

July 25th: Sopot – Poland
Don's diary: *"H borrowed my watch to go for a walk to the beach. We played here in Sopot again.... Good show..... All back to the hotel to eat and drink."*

July 26th: Kolobrzeg – Poland
Don's diary: *"I was up at 10:00am, had breakfast and packed to drive to Szczecin. Checked in the hotel.....ate and drank there. Night Off.*

July 27th: Don's diary: "I was still in bed at 1:00pm when Chas came round to borrow my hair brush (didn't know I had one). Nod came round for us to go and eat. Went for soundcheck. Good show. Came back to the hotel to clean up to do a press reception.

July 28th: Szczecin – Poland
Nod called me lunchtime to see if I wanted to go eat. I cleaned up, went for the sound check. GOOD gig. We all eat with the promoter at the hotel.

July 29th: Szczecin – Poland
Don's diary: *"Got up 9:00am. Cleaned up, went with the lighting crew to the gig. I wanted to sort my drums out. GOOD gig....All eat together at the hotel."*

July 30th: Bydgoszsz
Don's diary: *"I was up at 11:00am. Cleaned up and packed to drive to Bydgoszsz. Ate and drank in the hotel. I went to bed early. BUT, I was woken by Nod and JJ talking in the corridor to some American football players. ALSO, there was a 'sing-song' in the next room. People came from downstairs to complain."*

July 31st: Amfitear Zawisza, Bydgoszczy, Poland
Don's diary: *"I was wakened by traffic, stayed in bed until 12;00. Cleaned up, went for sound check and the concert - so-so show. We all eat in the hotel after."*

POLSKA AGENCJA ARTYSTYCZNA — „PAGART" WARSZAWA

PRZEDSIĘBIORSTWO IMPREZ ARTYSTYCZNYCH

„ESTRADA"

BYDGOSZCZ, UL. GRODZKA NR 7 • TEL. 222-096, 223-971

PREZENTUJE

NAJPOPULARNIEJSZĄ BRYTYJSKĄ GRUPĘ

Slade

TYLKO JEDEN KONCERT W BYDGOSZCZY
31 VII 1978 R. — GODZ. 19.00

AMFITEATR „ZAWISZA"

BILETY DO NABYCIA „ORBIS" ORAZ PIA „ESTRADA"

AUGUST 1978:

Tuesday 1st - Poznan – Poland
Support: Nick Van Eede
Don's diary: "The traffic woke me again 08:00. I stayed in bed until 09:00 when Micky Legg came round for his, socks, pants and boots...???????? I couldn't take a shower, the water was freezing. I went for breakfast before moving on to Torun. Not a very good show. I drank at the hotel later with Jim, Nick Eede (support act) and Chas. I had an early night."

Wednesday 2nd - Poznan – Poland
Support: Nick Van Eede
Don's diary: "I was awake early. BUT stayed in bed until 11:00. Called H to see if he wanted to go for breakfast. Our 'truckers' Mike & Paul were there. Mickey Legg joined us. I went for a sauna. H and our lighting crew were also there, Mickey Legg joined us. also Willi. I cleaned up, went to the hall to check my drums and do sound-check. GOOD SHOW. We all eat in the, hotel."

Thursday 3rd - Lodz – Poland,
Support: Nick Van Eede
Don's diary: *"Swinn called at 11:00am to say we would leave earlier. Checked out of the hotel and drove to Lodz. Checked in the hotel and went straight for sound-check. GOOD SHOW. Came back to the hotel. I drank with the roadies....."*

Friday 4th - Warzaw – Poland
Support: Nick Van Eede
Don's diary: "My alarm call came through at 09:00..... I cleaned up and packed, and went for breakfast before driving to Warsaw. Checked in the hotel. I did some laundry, had tea with H and Nick..... Went for the sound check. GOOD GIG... We all went to a disco after.??????"

Saturday 5th - Warzaw – Poland
Support: Nick Van Eede
Don's diary: *"I stayed in bed until 12:00..... I cleaned up and went for tea. Did an interview with an English reporter?????? Did our sound check,*

so-so show. Afterwards, we all went to a 'Jazz-Club'. Then drinks in the hotel."

Sunday 6th: Don's diary: "I was awake, 07:30, cleaned up, packed and went for, breakfast before driving to, 'Krakow'. DAY OFF. Checked in the hotel and ate there. Relaxed in the hotel all night, drinking."

Monday 7th - Krakow – Poland
Support: Nick Van Eede
Don's diary: "Stayed in bed until 1:00. Cleaned up. Apparently, some of our lighting crew 'mooned' out of the coach window to a religious procession (yesterday). We could be in 'BIG' trouble. Had a so-so show. Came back to the hotel and 'Jude' (lighting guy) drank in my room while we played music."

Tuesday 8th - Krakow – Poland
Support: Nick Van Eede
Don's diary: "I was awake at 08:00am, cleaned up and went for breakfast. Met the press for interviews..... I then had a walk round town before the sound check. GOOD SHOW. After, we all went to a 'jazz-club' to eat. I caught a cab back to our hotel."

Wednesday 9th - Krakow – Poland
Support: Nick Van Eede
Don's diary: "Stayed in bed until 11:00am. Cleaned up and went for breakfast. Had a walk round the town. Did sound check before a so-so show. Came back to the hotel for an early night."

Thursday 10th - Katowice – Poland
Support: Nick Van Eede
Don's diary: "I stayed in bed until 11:00am. Ordered tea to my room. Cleaned up to drive to Tarnow. Decent show. Came back to the hotel. Had a drink in Swinn's room before going to bed."

Friday 11th - Katowice – Poland
Support: Nick Van Eede

Don's diary: *"Got up, at 10:00 when my call came through. Cleaned up and packed... Went for breakfast before driving to Katowice. On the, way we went round AUSCHWITZ. George, our interpreter got so drunk, so he wouldn't have to go round. We found out later, he lost his family there. We checked in the hotel and relaxed all night."*

Saturday 12th - Opole – Poland
Support: Nick Van Eede
Don's diary: *"Stayed in bed until 12.00. Cleaned up and went downstairs to eat. Jim and myself did some shopping before the sound check. AMAZING CROWD. Went to a Russian Restaurant to eat. Spent the rest of the night in the hotel bar."*

Sunday 13th - Wroclaw – Poland
Support: Nick Van Eede
Don's diary: *"Stayed in bed until 10:30. Packed and drove to Opole. Checked in the hotel. Went for sound check. Did the show and drank in the hotel bar afterwards."*

Monday 14th: Wroclaw – Poland
Support: Nick Van Eede
Don's diary: *"Stayed in bed until 10:00am. Cleaned up, packed and drove to Wroclaw. Only a short drive. When we got there our truckers were very angry, as last night their passports had been stolen out of their trucks. They got them back straight away. We didn't ask any questions. I went to eat. H and Nick joined me for a sandwich. Had a great last show."*

15th: Don's diary: *"H rang to see if I wanted to go shopping and get rid of our Polish money. I got some 'flimsy' cymbals which bent when I put them in my suitcase, a 'penny whistle'. I gave the rest away..... I felt like Mother Teresa. Drank all night in the hotel bar."*

16th: The group flew back to London Heathrow airport.

20th: Rehearsals, Cannock.
21st: Rehearsals, Cannock.

Friday 25th – Withernsea Pavilion.
Don's diary: *"I was up at 09:00am. Cleaned up, packed and met Nod and Nick Van Eede at the office to drive to Withernsea. Did the sound-check. Nick had a real hard time with the audience. H's sister Carol was there with her husband and his family. After the show, we went to one of their mates' pub to drink for hours."*

Saturday 26th - West Runton Pavillion
Support: Nick Van Eede

Monday 28th - Stoneleigh Club, Porthcawl
Support: Nick Van Eede.

Don's diary: *"I was awake early. Cleaned up, caught a cab to Nod's. We drove to Porthcawl in Wales. Checked the equipment. Good show. BUT when we came off stage, a guy broke Nod's nose 'cause he was being rough with the kids down front and Nod told him to "clear-off"."*

..Noddy gets bashed

STOMPIN' rock star **Noddy Holder**, lead singer of the **Slade**, gave the tamest performance of his life last night.

With a broken nose, he wasn't taking any chances. Noddy, 27, was under doctor's orders to keep his head as still as possible.

The singer's nose was broken and both eyes blacked in a back-stage attack at a club in Porthcawl, Glamorgan, on Monday.

Noddy was taken to hospital for treatment and later made a statement to the police. But last night, he was back

By TOM MERRIN

on stage at a club in Cleethorpes, Lincs.

" My nose was broken for nothing," said Noddy " There were seven or eight hundred kids jumping about at the club when the bouncers started laying into them for no reason. I told the heavies to lay off — and

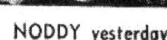

NODDY yesterday

one said: ' I'll see you later and show you how big I am.'

" I forgot about it, but when I was walking back to the dressing room, he just stepped out and lammed into me.

" I will still sing, although it may sound a bit thicker than usual."

Tuesday 29th - Bunny's Place. Grant Street, Cleethorpes
Support: Nick Van Eede
Don's diary: *"Swinn picked Nod and myself up to drive to Cleethorpes. GOOD SHOW."*

POP STAR BEATEN BY BOUNCER

Pop star Noddy Holder went on stage last night with a broken nose after a punch-up with a club bouncer. Noddy 28-year old singer with the Slade group, also had two black eyes. He was involved in a fracas with the bouncer the previous night at a disco in Porthcawl, South Wales.

Noddy who went on stage at Cleethorpes, Lincs, last night with his nose in a splint, said the trouble began when bouncers went on stage at the disco to hold back girl fans. He added: "The kids were ok but these bouncers got really heavy. One of them was punching the youngsters.

Claimed
Slade stopped playing and Noddy told the bouncers to clear off the stage. He claimed that one of them said "I'll get you afterwards."

Noddy said: "I told him he wasn't so big if he had to hit young girls. But I thought no more about it. I had just got to the dressing room door and this guy came up and hit me a right belter. I was flat on the floor before I knew what was happening.

Eyewitnesses said that one of Slade's managers and staff at the Stoneleigh Club separated the two men.

Hospital
Police were called and took Noddy to hospital at nearby Bridgend. Noddy and other members of the group went back to Porthcawl police station to make statements. Later he left for his home in Wolverhampton, West Midlands.

A police spokesman said "We are hoping to interview a man in connection with this incident."

BRIAN WESLEY

Pop star beaten up by concert bouncer

POP star Noddy Holder went on stage last night—with a broken nose and two black eyes.

The lead singer with top group Slade claims he had been punched by a bouncer after a concert at Porthcawl, South Wales, on Monday.

As he took to the stage at Cleethorpes, Lincolnshire, last night Mr Holder said: 'We had to go on because we do not like to disappoint the fans.'

Monday's incident happened after fans stormed the stage at Porthcawl and started to dance. Holder explained: 'The bouncers came on and started laying into them rather heavily. 'It seemed to be developing into a bloodbath, so I told the bouncers to get off and leave them alone.

'One of them turned round and told me: 'I will get you later.

'I thought nothing more about it, but at the end of the show as I was walking off stage, he just stepped out of the darkness and laid me flat.

'I have made a statement to police, and they are following it up.

After last night's two shows he added: 'My nose did start bleeding at one stage, but I managed to get through all right.

DAILY EXPRESS Tuesday July 3 1979

Bouncer broke my nose claims Noddy

EXPRESS REPORTER

A RAVE-UP at a pop concert ended with singer Noddy Holder of "Slade" nursing a broken nose, a court heard yesterday. It was all due to club bouncers being too aggressive with fans, the 29-year-old pop star claimed.

He told Cardiff Crown Court that the stewards were creating a bad atmosphere by pushing people around.

He said to one of them over a microphone : "You must be a big boy taking on people half your size."

It was alleged the man replied : "Call me what you like—I'll see you later."

Holder described his group's performance as "very riotous."

Fell

When the show at the Stoneleigh Club, Porthcawl, Glamorgan, was over, Holder said a man approached him backstage, put his arm around his shoulder and said : "I'm the big boy who talked to you."

When Holder replied : "Yeah," the man punched him on the nose.

Said Holder : "I fell to the floor. All I can remember is that he was a dark, broad-shouldered fellow."

Holder, of Chelsea Embankment, London, was giving evidence against club steward Desmond Brothers, who is charged with inflicting grievous bodily harm on him.

Brothers, aged 29, of Pyle, Glamorgan, denies the charge. The hearing continues.

NODDY HOLDER
Broken nose

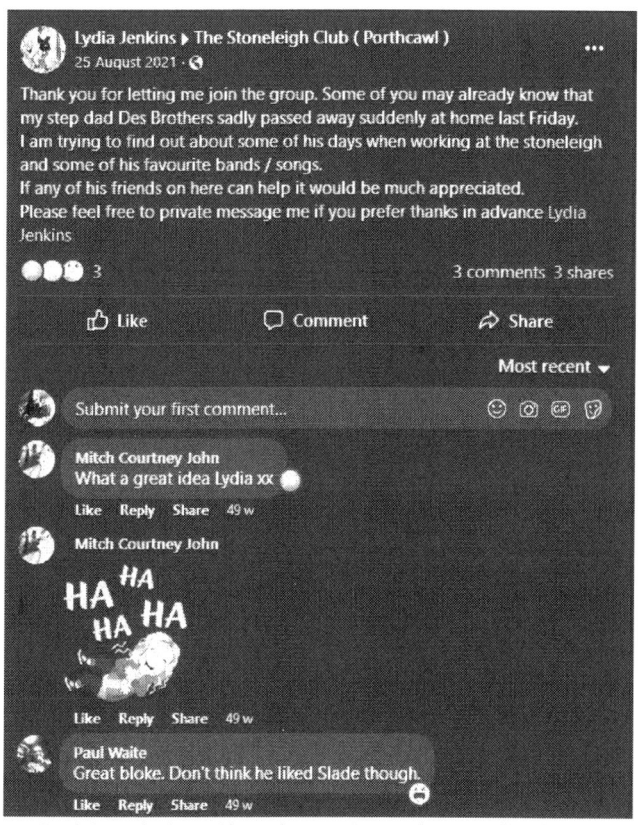

As a postscript to what must have been a traumatic event for all concerned...

Sian Lewis
This was not what I saw! Noddy called all the fans up on stage! and then it turned into a riot! my friends girl had to go to hospital after someone fell on her, there were people falling off the stage and total chaos! and Noddy looked terrified, and wanted protection from the bouncers! hence they were angry with Noddy! he had encouraged the fans up, and had caused the riot! and then he wanted protection. Gareth

Wednesday 30th – Bunny's Place. Grant Street, Cleethorpes.

Don's diary: *"Reception called to say we had to check out. Did the sound check before going to the Police Station to make statements about the 'punch-up' in Porthcawl. We had a good show. Nod and myself drove to London with Nick Van Eede and his driver Nick........"*

SEPTEMBER 1978

Slade

SLADE have an extensive six-week schedule lined up through the first part of the autumn, playing Chatham Central Hall (September 23), Watford Bailey's (24-30), Leicester Bailey's (October 2-7), Southport New Theatre (8), Blackburn Bailey's (9-14), Keele University (18), Newcastle Polytechnic (20), Nottingham University (21), Carlisle Market Hall (22), Sheffield Polytechnic (23), Weston-super-Mare Webbington Club (25), Reading University (26), Guildford Surrey University (27), Bradford University (28), Derby Assembly Rooms (29) and Warrington Wilderspool Leisure Centre (November 1). Support act is singer-composer Nick van Eede, a new discovery of Slade manager Chas Chandler.

September 9th 1978:
Recording Studio. Mixing tracks.

17th:
Recording Studio. Selecting new single.

18th: Rehearsals.

Saturday 23rd
Central Hall Chatham
Support: Nick Van Eede
Don's diary described the gig as "a good first show."

Sunday 24th
Baileys Nightclub,
Watford
Support: Nick Van Eede

Monday 25th: Baileys Nightclub, Watford
Support: Nick Van Eede

Tuesday 26th September 1978 - Baileys Nightclub – Watford
Support: Nick Van Eede
Don described it as 'a good show' in his diary.

September 27th 1978:
Don went to the group's office to do some interviews with 'Newsbeat'.
Baileys Nightclub – Watford
Support: Nick Van Eede
Don described the show as 'so-so' in his diary.

Thursday 28th - Baileys Nightclub – Watford
Support: Nick Van Eede

Friday 29th - Baileys Nightclub – Watford
Support: Nick Van Eede

Saturday 30th - Baileys Nightclub – Watford.
Support: Nick Van Eede

OCTOBER 1978

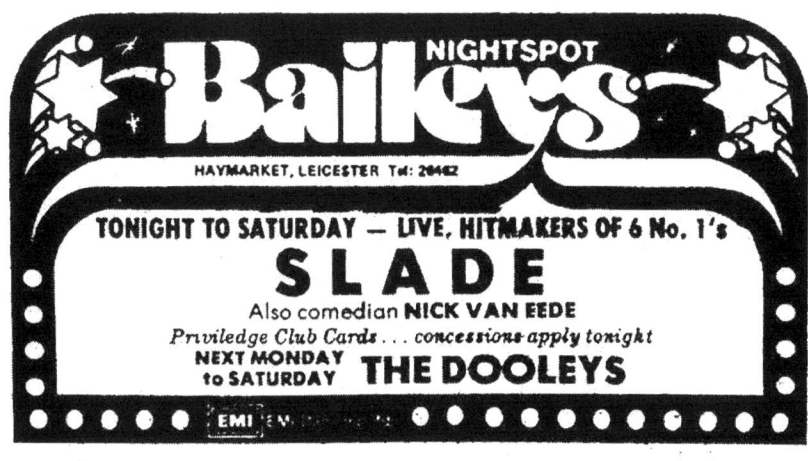

Slade with comedian Nick Van Eede?

Monday 2nd - Baileys Nightclub. Haymarket, Leicester
Support: Nick Van Eede

Tuesday 3rd - Baileys Nightclub. Haymarket, Leicester
Support: Nick Van Eede

Wednesday 4th - Baileys Nightclub. Haymarket, Leicester
Support: Nick Van Eede

Thursday 5th - Baileys Nightclub. Haymarket, Leicester
Support: Nick Van Eede

Friday 6th - Baileys Nightclub. Haymarket, Leicester
Support: Nick Van Eede

Saturday 7th - Baileys Nightclub. Haymarket, Leicester
Support: Nick Van Eede

Sunday 8th - Southport Theatre, The Promenade.
Support: Nick Van Eede

SUNDAY OCTOBER 8
7.30

SLADE

250p, 225p, 150p, 125p

Audio of this show exists. A number of the crowd invaded the stage, despite several requests from the group not to do so. They climbed over a cover that went across the orchestra pit, which was not made to take the weight of people and inevitably, it collapsed, leading to the show being cut short. The same skinhead "fans" from Liverpool were seen mugging other fans outside the venue after the show.

Monday 9th
Cavendish Club. Lord Sq, Blackburn
Support: Nick Van Eede

Tuesday 10th
Cavendish Club, Lord Sq, Blackburn
Support: Nick Van Eede

Wednesday 11th
Cavendish Club. Lord Sq, Blackburn
Support: Nick Van Eede
Blackburn Students Union Freshers Ball

Blackburn's Student Union
present their
FRESHERS BALL
Wednesday, 11th Oct.
at
The Cavendish Club
8 p.m. - 2 a.m.
with SLADE
Tickets 50p at Ames Records and Student Union or £1 at the door.
NO DRESS RESTRICTIONS.

Thursday 12th:
Their show at the Cavendish Club, Blackburn was cancelled as Dave Hill had burned himself at home, trying to light a fire in the garden with petrol to burn some rubbish.

One of the newspapers helpfully wrote that he should have had an ADULT with him. Another music paper suggested that the rubbish was *recent Slade recordings…*

Guitarist injured in garden fire

Pop group Slade were unable to appear at Blackburn's Cavendish last night after lead guitarist Dave Hill was burned in a petrol fire.

Dave was in the garden of his Wolverhampton home lighting a bonfire with some petrol when flames burned his arm. The group will be back on stage tonight.

Friday 13th - Cavendish Club. Lord Square, Blackburn After the show, the group all drove to Newcastle and checked in the hotel for Chas Chandler & Madeline's wedding the next day.

Rock And Roll Bolero / It's Alright Buy Me single released on Barn 2014127.

This song was originally called 'I've Been Rejected' and the recording featured Jim Lea on violin, making for an almost ELO-sounding track. The single sadly did not chart. Many fans thought that the B-side was a far superior song to the A-side.

Jim Lea later said to the Fan Club: *"The comment on Rock n Roll Bolero is that it was different for Slade, but it was ordinary compared to everything else that was going around at the time. But I really dig the record myself! You see, when we walk on stage we can rip the arse off straight rock, but we can't do the same* with "Rock 'n' Roll Bolero". It's great on record, but it's us thinking, it's not us being ourselves."

Melody Maker: *"Same as ever, apart from the syn drum, sole concession to modernity. How can a group who strung so many hits together a few years back fade so completely? It wasn't them who changed, so it must be us. Someone painted on a corrugated fence by Vauxhall Bridge: Whatever happened to Slade? Another brush added: Slik took over. Whatever happened to Slik?"*

Sounds: *"A doctor writes: the position that Slade occupy these days in the sad netherworld of pop's wasteland has a reservation or ten already booked for the current TOTPunks in a few years' time. The symptoms remain the same – the string of hit singles; the lengthy unsuccessful hammering away at Uncle Sam's 24-carat door while the homeland fans move onto other things (rock bands living forever, but not so little boys, pogoing and phlegm propulsion soon making way for other toys); predictable talk of getting more involved in the moving pictures field; the life support machine of fading past glories. Slade seem subdued, Noddy himself is so mellowed that I look forward to the band covering "Christmas (War is over)" and any song that rips of Ravel for their hook line punch has got to be a load of cobblers. After influencing more 70's songwriters (count 'em) than any other musicians, it's too bad."*

Saturday 14th

The group attended Chas Chandler & Madeline's wedding, then went back to play at the Cavendish Club. Lord Square, Blackburn. Support: Nick Van Eede.

The club was later destroyed by a fire.

Wednesday 18th - Keele University,
Support: Nick Van Eede

Thursday 19th - Nod and Don drove to Sheffield to appear on a radio show.

Friday 20th - Newcastle Poly

**Newcastle Poly Ents. presents
on Friday, 20th October, 1978**

SLADE

plus Support & Disco   Late Bar
Doors open 8 p.m.

All persons must either have a valid union card or to be signed into the building by a bonafide student member.

**Advance Tickets £1.30
£1.50 on door**

№ 581

Saturday 21st - Nottingham University.
(Nod and Jim did a local radio interview earlier in the day)

Monday 22nd - Market Hall, Carlisle

Monday 23rd - Polytechnic. Phoenix Building, Pond St, Sheffield
Support: Nick Van Eede

Sheffield City Polytechnic
Students' Union
RAG COMMITTEE

N⁰ 361

presents the

Rag Ball '78

featuring **SLADE**

NICK VAN EEDE   **DISCO**

MONDAY, 23rd OCTOBER, 8.00 p.m. 'til late
THE PHOENIX HALL, Pond Street

Tickets: In advance £1·40   On the door £1·60
LATE BAR   R.O.A.R.

SHEFFIELD STUDENTS' RAG

POLYTECHNIC RAG BALL

featuring

SLADE

plus support on
MONDAY, OCT. 23rd,
8.30 p.m.

Tickets £1.40 advance,
£1.60 on door.
Late Bar
Members and bona fide
guests only.

Wednesday 25th - Webbington Country Club, Weston Super Mare
Support: Paper Lace

Audio of this show exists:
1. Dizzy Mama
2. Night Starvation
3. Take Me Bak 'Ome
4. Wheels Ain't Coming Down
5. Lemme Love Into Ya
6. Everyday
7. Something Else Medley
8. When I'm Dancin' I Ain't Fightin'
9. Gudbuy T' Jane
10. Get Down & Get With It
11. You'll Never Walk Alone
12. Cum On Feel The Noize
13. I'm A Rocker
14. Born To Be Wild

Thursday 26th – Radio show Reading (Nod / Don) University, Reading

SLADE

SLADE

SLADE, currently in the middle of their UK tour, will be playing an additional gig at the London Music Machine on October 30. The band had to cancel their October 12 concert at Bailey's Club Blackburn because guitarist Dave Hill was injured in a domestic accident. Dave was taken to hospital and treated for forearm burns and Slade played the gig the following day. Dates are now as follows: Guildford University October 27, Bradford University 28, Derby Assembly Rooms 29, London Music Machine 30.

Friday 27th – University, Guildford, Surrey

SURREY UNIVERSITY
S.U. PRESENTS

 *SLADE*

Friday 27th October 1978   8.00 p.m.

Nº 269

£1.75 Advance   £2.00 Door

Slade Alive Vol Two album released. Barn 2314106.

Get On Up / Take Me Bak 'Ome / My Baby Left Me / Be / Mama Weer All Crazee Now / Burnin' In The Heat Of Love / Everyday / Gudbuy T' Jane / One-Eyed Jacks / C'mon Feel The Noize

POLYDOR PUSH FOR NEW SLADE ALBUM.
An extensive campaign is being mounted by Polydor to promote Slade's new album Slade Alive Volume Two, released to coincide with a concert tour which takes in Newcastle, Nottingham, Sheffield, Reading, London and Liverpool. These venues will be hit by a flyposting campaign, with 5000, four-colour posters featuring the slogan "More Alive Than You'd Believe". Full page ads are being taken in Music Week and Melody Maker, while 1000 four colour posters are available to dealers for window and in-store displays.

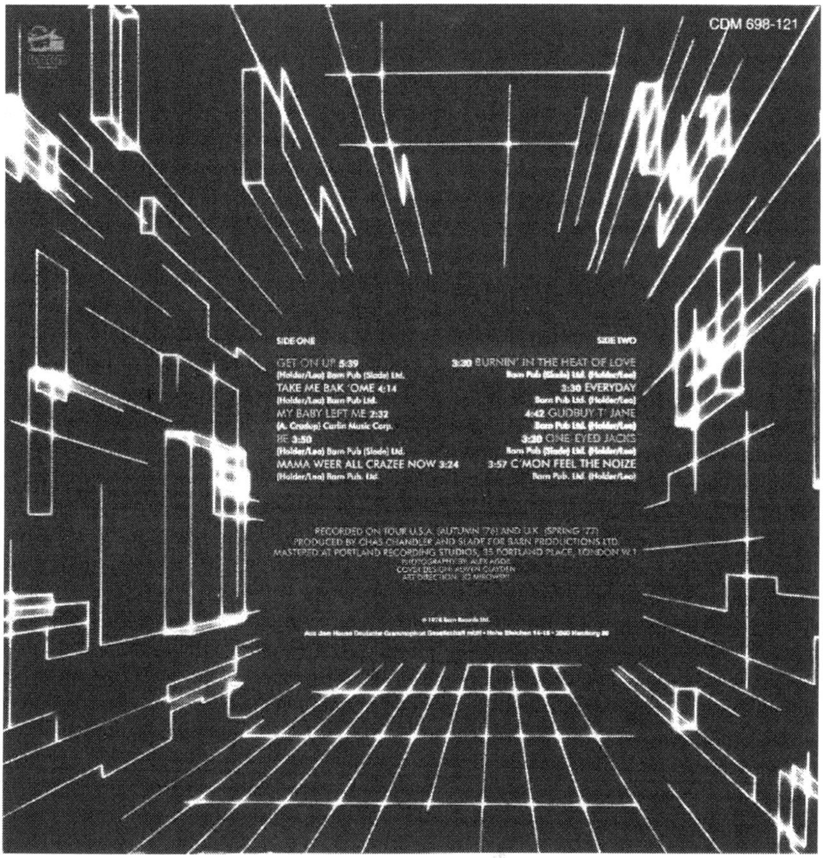

SIDE ONE
GET ON UP 5:39
(Holder/Lea) Barn Pub (Slade) Ltd.
TAKE ME BAK 'OME 4:14
(Holder/Lea) Barn Pub Ltd.
MY BABY LEFT ME 2:32
(A. Crudup) Carlin Music Corp.
BE 3:50
(Holder/Lea) Barn Pub (Slade) Ltd.
MAMA WEER ALL CRAZEE NOW 3:24
(Holder/Lea) Barn Pub. Ltd.

SIDE TWO
3:20 BURNIN' IN THE HEAT OF LOVE
Barn Pub (Slade) Ltd. (Holder/Lea)
3:30 EVERYDAY
Barn Pub Ltd. (Holder/Lea)
4:42 GUDBUY T' JANE
Barn Pub Ltd. (Holder/Lea)
3:20 ONE-EYED JACKS
Barn Pub (Slade) Ltd. (Holder/Lea)
3:57 C'MON FEEL THE NOIZE
Barn Pub. Ltd. (Holder/Lea)

RECORDED ON TOUR U.S.A. (AUTUMN '76) AND U.K. (SPRING '77)
PRODUCED BY CHAS CHANDLER AND SLADE FOR BARN PRODUCTIONS LTD.
MASTERED AT PORTLAND RECORDING STUDIOS, 35 PORTLAND PLACE, LONDON W.1
PHOTOGRAPHY BY ALEX AGOR
COVER DESIGN: ASPEN GUYATT
ART DIRECTION: JO MISCHWEN

SLADE ALIVE Vol. II

Its been 18 months now since Slade released their last LP. "Whatever happened to Slade" and a lot has happened since then. Slade have been one of the busiest 'live' bands on the scene recently and this LP shows exactly what is actually going on, a group that were so big just a few years ago, with number one hits, here, there and everywhere. Somewhat unknown today seems very strange, but times change and believe it or not Slade have. On this LP not only do we hear early rockers, like Gudbye t'Jane, but such songs like "Burning in the heat of love" and "Be" a great, heavy rocker, along with songs like Crudups hit "My baby left me" and some early songs. Slade present us with a neat little package! One complaint though, they did not include their recent single "Rock N Roll Bolero" a classic no doubt, oh well, we can't expect too much can we? ****   K. Massey

The advert in music papers said "MORE ALIVE THAN YOU'D BELIEVE." *The sleeve states that the album came from recordings made on their USA tour in 1976 and their British tour in 1977 (the final Ipswich show).*

It later came out that some of the songs were actually recorded in live sessions at Portland Studios and that crowd noise was dubbed onto the recordings for atmosphere.

Saturday 28th – University, Bradford
Support: Nick Van Eede.
According to Don's diary, Nick had to go to hospital for a check-up.

Jim and Don with fans outside the University.

SLADE
At the Great Hall

BRADFORD UNIVERSITY, 28/10/78
Whatever happened to Slade? The question was answered before a packed house at Bradford University. The answer being pure and simple, that the noise makers are back on the British scene and are playing better than ever before.

Despite the lack of success chartwise with recent record releases the group gradually worked the audience into a frenzy. The opening number, "Hear Me Calling" proved that Slade are back in business, the audience at the front of the stage were crushed by the sheer force of people behind trying to push forward. Also the Student Union bouncers had to put up with the tedious business of trying to restrain certain fanatical members of the audience clambering on stage.

Slade combined a mixture of their old hits (or "oldies but goodies" as singer Noddy Holder referred to them) such as "Gudbuy T'Jane", "Far Far Away" and "Everyday" with new material such as the group's new single "Rock'n'Roll Bolero" (a must for the charts) and the excellent violin solo performed by Jim Lea, showing what craftsmen the group have become since their glitter-bop days.

Slade closed the show performing three encores, but they still left the audience unsatisfied. The last time Slade played in Bradford was in 1974 at the St. George's Hall, then they brought the house down by reputation alone, this time they still acommplished the feat, but they had to win the audience over — making the concert more of a success for the group than before.

David Kemp

SEPTEMBER

Fri. 29th	"Gang of 4"	CB
Sat. 30th	Supercharge	CB

OCTOBER

Mon. 2nd	Bernard Wrigley	CB
Mon. 2nd	Phonogram Disco	GH
Wed. 4th	Climax Blues Band	GH
Fri. 6th	Steel Band	CB
Sat. 7th	Camel	GH
Wed. 11th	Wilko Johnson's Solid Senders	CB
Sat. 14th	Jab Jab/90° Inclusive	GH
Sun. 15th	Steel Pulse	GH
Wed. 18th	Whirlwind	CB
Sat. 21st	Radio Stars	GH
Wed. 25th	Wire	CB
Sat. 28th	Slade	GH

NOVEMBER

Wed. 1st	Dire Straights	CB
Fri. 3rd	bonfire Spectacular	CB
Wed. 8th	Pirates	CB
Fri. 10th	Afwoodly Jets	CB
Sat. 11th	Pyjama Romp	GH
Wed. 15th	Bethnal	CB
Fri. 17th	Red Ladder Theatre	CB
Sat. 18th	To be confirmed	
Wed. 22nd	Fabulous Poodles	CB
Sat. 25th	The Rezillos	GH
Wed. 29th	Punishment of Luxury	CB

DECEMBER

Sat. 2nd	Mud	GH
Wed. 6th	"Three Four"	CB

Sunday 29th - Assembly Rooms. Market Place, Derby
Support: Nick Van Eede

Monday 30th - Music Machine. High Street, Camden, London
Support: Nick Van Eede

MUSIC MACHINE
CAMDEN HIGH STREET

MONDAY, 30th OCTOBER, 1978

SLADE

Plus Special Guest

ON STAGE MIDNIGHT

Doors open 8.00 p.m.

Tickets £2.50

No 0377

MUSIC MACHINE

TELEPHONE 01-387-0428/9

CAMDEN HIGH ST. OPP. MORNINGTON CRESCENT TUBE N.W.1

Wednesday 20th
TRADITION
plus Fusion
Admission £1.00

Monday ¼ × TH
CHELSEA
Plus The Fall
Plus Snivellin' Shits
Admission £1.00

Thursday 21st
HI-TENSION
plus Abbraka
Advanced Tickets £2.00 From Box Office

£Tuesday 26th
THE JOLT
Plus Hollywood Killers
Admission £1.00

Friday 22nd
SANDY AND THE BACKLINE
Plus Showbiz Kids
Admission £2.00

Wednesday 27th
SORE THROAT
plus The Vye
Admission £1.00

Monday 16th October
THE PIRATES
Advance Tickets £2.00 From Box Office

Saturday 23rd
GONZALEZ
plus support
Admission £2.00

Monday 30th October
SLADE
Advance Tickets £2.50 From Box Office

LICENSED BARS – LIVE MUSIC – DANCING
8PM – 2 AM   MONDAY TO SATURDAY

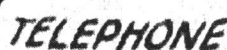

Slade

Music Machine

Hitless for so long, I feared Slade would surely be parody or travesty, caricature Rude Boyz en route for Batley Variety Club.

Not this century. Noddy Holder's voice could separate scampi from breadcrumbs at a hundred paces and apart from the odd *bon mot* — "Jim and I were sitting on the banks of the Mississippi, watching the turds float by" — the smut count was low.

Starting with Alvin Lee's "Hear Me Calling", Slade gave a totally authoritative display of rock 'n roll rifferama.

"Coz I Luv You" and "Merry Christmas Everybody", two of their biggest hits, were surprisingly omitted but we got most of the rest. (They'd be listed here if I could remember how to mis-spell them.)

Whether on the quintessentially Wolverhampton wistfulness of "Everyday" or the shotgun marriage of "That's All Right Mama" and "My Baby Left Me", the Slade stamp is unmistakable. A more objective producer than longtime svengali Chas Chandler might be the catalyst to channel this individuality into new areas.

Jimmy Lea is probably the best musician and gets solo spots on bass and fiddle, proving more entertaining on the latter. But Slade are a unit, with Lea providing the fluid, melodic element just as John Entwistle does with the Who.

The crash-bang-wallop element comes courtesy of Don Powell, the John Snow of the kit.

Slade already make Sham 69 look extremely silly. With a hit single and album they'd leave most mainstream rockers so far down the field you'd have to pump air into 'em.

Harry George

A short-lived Slade fanzine named SLAYED carried an interview.

Slade recently returned to Britain after an absence of some two years to find that their devoted fans had grown up and they had been forgotten. Instead of fading into obscurity they decided to start again - at the beginning, playing all over the country in small clubs. It was in one of these that a surprisingly optimistic Dave Hill told us why they had stayed away for so long and how they were strategically planning a comeback.

How's the tour going and why are you playing small clubs rather than big halls?

Well we've done about seven dates so far and the object is to get to more people. The trouble is that a lot of people think that we're still in America and everytime we release a record we get slagged off so we thought the best thing to do was get out on the road and show 'em that we're 'ere. We're trying to get to the people the way we started and build up a following again. We've got a basic following anyway which we haven't lost but obviously we're not as big as we used to be because of the lack of hit singles you know but we're mainly a working band and we feel our strongest point is getting out to people and playing. We're not feeling down about playing smaller places. We're really enjoying it.

If you do a smaller place you don't come under so much pressure and the whole set is much looser.

Did you ever regret going to America for so long?

In some aspects yes. Obviously we've lost a certain amount of ground in Britain but also we have gained something. We went to America to try and improve ourselves because we were getting a bit complaisant. We wished that we hadn't gone for so long but more than anything, the Press over here said we'd gone for tax reasons and that we'd quit and all that crap but we paid our tax.

What did you think of America?

Yes we thought it was a good place but not as good as England to play but youre playing to a lot of foreigners aint ya in America. They have a different sort of feel towards you. Your act tends to get longer and becomes different but we think a little bit of America has helped us but getting back here we'll get back to the nitty and gritty again. Even in the last album you can see the change. It wasn't a successful album but we thought it was better musically.

We thought that things kinda started to slow down after you played Earls Court ...

We thought we were exhausting the market actually. They were seeing too much of us. You know when it seems like you can get too much of a good thing.

Do you think that most of the people who went to see you at the Rainbow went more out of curiousity than anything else?

Yes right. James Hunt was there. I mean I never knew he was a fan. That's strange innit. He turns up and buys a ticket at the front door. He didn't sorta ask for a pass he just turned up like a regular person and he just bought a ticket on the door and I was flabbergasted. Brought him round the dressing room and he was pissed as arseholes you know. He said it's going to be a rave is it. He just wanted to see the aggravation. Being a racing driver he just thought where's the excitement you know. So he came for a bit of fun you know, which I think a lot of has gone out of the business since we've been away. You ve had punk come up and all that but I think there's a lot of aggravation which has been around for some time, which has been biting at the people. There's noone catering for the fun element anymore.

What were the audiences like in America?

Very much like the Status Quo boogie-type audiences we get over here. We've got a following but they're more into the words than the songs. They always check the words out and try to find out what you're all about. They call us a "kick ass" band, a boozy band and we're not trying to be ultra cool and in places like St Louis we've become very big (we drew 10,000 last time we played there). The Press in America very very anti us because of our success here. We had such a big build up that people were saying we were bigger than the Beatles and, therefore, the kids were very wary of us because naturally they didn't want to be hyped. So they kinda expected too much from us at first. Unfortunately we were stuck right at the top of the bill at big halls and not selling out and the press were just cutting us up with knives you know. It took us ages to live that down.

Were you shocked at the audience reaction at the Rainbow? You did five encores didnt you?

Yes, that's the most we've ever done in our lives. We were obviously very pleased. Noddy had got a sore throat that night and he was working his arse off to get it right. We were very surpised at the over all reaction to that gig because the audience were by far wilder than I thought they were going to be. Actually I thought they might be a bit laid back. I mean even the press seemed to notice that. It was like being caught in a time warp, almost as if we'd never been away.

What is the purpose of this tour, because you have no record to push at the moment?

We're on the road to suss out what's going on and for us it's playing. I don't want to sit at home, I want to be playing. We have a live album coming out though, "Slade Alive II" which is finished just about but we hope to build up the following and then bring it out.

We don't want to stay off the road and say we'll do a tour to promote an album. You see we do this kind of tour so that we can keep working. I'm sure a lot of punk kids would get off on us. If anyone knows rock music we should because we're old enough to know it.

Well you can reckon on "Merry Christmas Everybody" being released every year ..

We actually made it in New York in the heat of the August summer and the feeling we got on the record was really Christmasy. I don't know how the hell we pulled that off. It was stinking hot in New York and it's a horrible place to be anyway and we were making a Christmas record! I wasn't very sure about it actually but the nearer it got to Christmas the better it sounded.

At this moment the door was opened by a very enebriated Chas Chandler who dragged Dave Hill away.

Sadly only time will tell whether Slade will once again rule the charts (preferably album) but here's hoping!

NOVEMBER 1978

1st
Wilderspool Leisure Centre, Warrington

2nd
IBC studio - recording

3rd
IBC studio - recording

4th
Nod and Don drove to Portsmouth for a radio show.

6th
IBC studio - recording

7th
IBC studio - recording "Don't Waste Your Time".

8th
IBC studio - recording overdubs.

9th
IBC studio - recording 'an Elvis Costello style reggae song'.

13th
Don went to Brighton to see Chas's new signings The Depressions.

21st:
Don went to the studio to put tambourine on Nick Van Eede's new track "Rock n' Roll' Fool". The track was used as the A-side of a single BARN 2014 128, coupled with the song Ounce Of Sense.

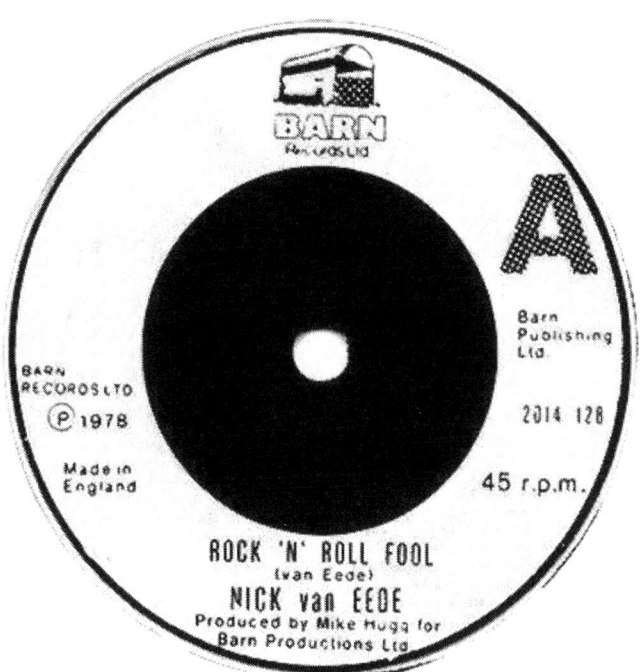

Sunday 26th - Rehearsals, Wolverhampton.

(Slade's show at The Mayflower Club, Birch Street, Manchester was cancelled, at short notice as the venue had recently closed down).

THE MAYFLOWER CLUB
1/3 BIRCH STREET, OFF HYDE ROAD MANCHESTER

Thursday November 9th
IAN GILLAN BAND
+ Support

Friday November 10th
SKREWDRIVER
+ Guests Bitch

Saturday November 11th
GLORIA MUNDI
+ from Holland
One Way Subway

Sunday November 12th
SENSATIONAL ALEX HARVEY BAND
(with Alex Harvey)

Friday November 17th
PURE HELL
(From America, the worlds first all black punk band)

Saturday November 18th
JAPAN
+ Support

Sunday November 19th
MERGER
+ Support

Wednesday November 22nd
THE CONTENDERS
(with Jim Capaldi)

Thursday November 23rd
STADIUM DOGS
+ Support

Friday November 24th
SNIPS
+ Support

Saturday November 25th
DAVID JOHANSEN BAND
(Ex N.Y. Dolls)
+ Support

Sunday November 26th
SLADE
+ Special Guests
Skrewdriver

Thursday November 30th
SQUEEZE
+ Support

Friday December 1st
DAVE LEWIS BAND
Featuring Charlie McCracken (Ex Taste)
& Rob Townshend (Ex Family)

Tickets available from Virgin Records, tel 061 236 4801. Piccadilly Records, tel 061 236 2555. Paperchase, tel. 061-834 7992. One Stop, tel 061 236 8314 & Discland, tel 061 624 4904. Or from club. Further enquiries ring 061 624 1174.

27th: Cardiff.

28th: Norwich.

Wednesday 29th - Great British Music Festival - Wembley, London
Slade were mid-bill, appearing along with The Jam / The Pirates / Generation X

Mel Bush presents

Wednesday 29th November

THE JAM
GENERATION X
SLADE
THE PIRATES
PATRIK FITZGERALD
BERNIE TORME
Nicky Horne

The Great British Music Festival at Wembley Arena 1978

GREAT BRITISH MUSIC FESTIVAL, Wembley Arena. Day One

WHAT A jolly old way for all the consciously street-reared to spend a night: to roll up, blow a fiver on yer ticket, eighty pee on a programme, select your T-shirt, sweat-shirt, badge, poster, remnant, souvenir, keepsake. The world of the big glamour biz banks at the wave's expense, at your expense, at its leisure.

Wembley Empire Pool sucks as a venue for anything musical, a far cry from Dingwalls or the Marquee. On this occasion, it remains little more than half-full, and most of the occupants seem to be police; when Paul Weller says "We're gonna do a love song now, and if any of you are laughing, someone was stabbed tonight . . ." before launching into 'I Need You', the audience bows into a deathly, ironic hush. And the response is genuine. Paul Weller, being Paul Weller, doesn't push the point.

The Great British Music Festival. The Great British crowd violence we all know, love and can't do without . . . From what I saw, this event was a triumph for the Jam, a triumph for Slade. And Generation X were aw-ful.

By the time I arrived, Berni Torme, Patrik Fitzgerald and The Pirates had been hastily ushered on / off stage, and Slade were blasting through 'My Baby Left Me'. I've never liked Noddy Holder's head-splitting voice and this was painful nostalgia, kinda funny to see all those scarves and arms waving about, the halcyon days of the teeny-boom. On top of that, Slade piled oodles of solos, jams, lighting effects and daft raps about how "you paid yer f----g money, so have a good time!"

A best of Slade night. The new material don't exactly bomb, but it's pretty redundant nevertheless.

'Take Me Bak Ome', 'Goodbuy t' Jane', 'Mama Weer All Crazee Now' . . . this band's reliance on old faves is pretty astounding, pretty frightening. And when Noddy, on 'Get Down Get With It', sings "Let your hair daaaarn" to the skin-headed hoards, you (or I) just gotta laugh.

They are powerful, they do have great visual impact, they are successful in their mission. The multitudes lap 'em up, and though I didn't get off on 'em at all, that hardly matters.

THE OPENING night of last week's Great British Music Festival was bad enough, what with the souvenir gimmickry, the inflated drink prices and the fact that the bars closed around 9.30. Add to that the continuous running mods - versus - skins battles (Jam fans / Slade fans) and you get one big flop.

Great British Music Festival
Wembley Arena

Meanwhile, belching is back in vogue. Slade, surprisingly, don't thow custard pies at one another. They straddle amps, wave their willies about, play "Born To Be Wild". THEY ARE BACK! What a great bloody bunch of lads, eh?

NEW MUSICAL EXPRESS

The Jam/Generation X/Slade/The Pirates
Wembley

WE FREE ourselves from football heads and make for the rock and roll. Every road leads to Wembley. Or so the ticket says. It was just like going to a football match on a darkly grim Wednesday night, getting out of work early an' all. I've missed Patrick Thingy and Bernie Thingy. Oh how sad but never mind.

You need a compass to find your seat and I feel really chuffed with myself when I do locate the correct spot. The Pirates (all this time) have been confusing me. Who CAN that racket be? Well, you can imagine some of the names that were sprinting through my mind in response. Suffice to say they were severely duff enough to have me speculating whether the dreaded Slade could beat this for audio and visual atrocities against the person?

If you've seen this latter band recently and you aren't Noddy Flask's mummy you already know the answer. They really are BAAD. *"Waay! Yew bewgers!"* Meg Richardson rock with a vengeance, and there is no escape. They exploit the lowest common denominators possible in terms of songs and crowd teasing and I hate them for it. They must go.

We try and recover from the holocaust, but the beer's dreadful and the atmosphere's worse. It's like a neverending toilet without flush facilities, and the gangs are hanging around searching for a bundle, mods, very impressive I must say satorially, in parkas (is that the correct term? I'm so uncool!) and skins in, well, skins clobber.

I'm uncomfortable. Cold. Frightened. Slightly lost. And there are girls yelling "Billy"! Only the odd retreating Slade case, edging another inch to the asylum, another inch to West Bromwich. Across the stage a massive (well, it was FAIRLY big) curtain shields a non-existent Bruce Forsyth. Gen X sweep embarrassingly on stage. Woops! Sorry Tony! I nearly forgot you're *stars* now. Billy's fat and ugly while Tony looks like a deformed orangutang in his leathers and libido. Hooray!

'Ready Steady Gooo!' opens the set. It's so appaling I can't believe this is the band that made one of the best albums of 1978.

The sound is seriously sloppy, and surely the band themselves can't be at all happy with this level of performance. The new songs sound uniformly atrocious. The whole set was a disaster from beginning to end, and yet they had the nerve to stand up there and veritably GLOAT in their own self abasement.

For the record, the new songs included 'Night Of The Cadillacs' ('Born To Be Wild' on a Hoover) and 'The English Gene' (aah!). Dinky toy drumming, the slowest, most cumbersome guitar work I've heard all year, god they should be ashamed of themselves. And I'm SERIOUS. It took me a long time to recover from that catastrophe, but the general consensus was one of how CAN the Jam hope to retrieve anything from the debris of the preceding four hours dross. More fool us. The Rickenbacker trio taught us all a lesson. And how!

'All Mod Cons' opened the proceedings. The sound was perfect, leaving it all up to Weller and his trusty blade and he came through it like a god. They went on to provide what was probably one of the best live performances I've seen all year. They bordered on the flawless at times. 'Mr. Clean' was one of a whole set of undoubted stand-outs, Weller's guitar cutting and decisive, like striking a match over a ragged brick wall. Visually, they weren't at all lost on the large Daily Censor stage, Foxton and Weller using every inch to full effect. Moreover, the old songs combined superbly with the material from the new album, 'Away From The Numbers' for instance coming across powerful and terribly threatening. It was so unusual seeing a band that actually MEANT it, man, y'know?

'News Of The World' (you card Weller!) scratched pieces out of the night in anger. Weller is so emotionally intense and spontaneous on stage it's almost impossible not being swept along on the angry surf. 'Down In The Tube Station' featured subway sound effects and sounded every bit the mighty song that it is. And all so relevant on that chilly night when a member of the audience was stabbed in the name of rock and roll. You stupid cunts. The music reflected the bite and mood of the night and the power was simply awesome. The Jam in my estimation scrawled their name on the rugged stone of rock and roll that night. These are moments when the music reached beyond aural entertainment. This was one of those moments. Thank you Weller, Foxton and Buckler. . .   *DAVE McCULLOUGH*

30th:
Photo session with Robert Ellis at Slade's offices.

DECEMBER 1978

REVIEWED BY BOB GELDOF, who used to be NME's Dublin correspondent but joined The Boomtown Rats because the money was better.

SLADE: Merry Xmas Everybody / Don't Blame Me (Polydor). About its fourth time up, this one. Whatever happened to Christmas? Slade put the boot back into it, that's wot. One of our (The Boomtown Rats) favourite single bands. I love it. Everybody else will hate it.

1st: CARDIFF STUDENTS GIG.
Don's diary: *"Willi, Nod and myself drove to Cardiff. Good gig. Swinn said we should buy the crew something for Christmas. I said "a Slade CD". Drove home after."*

2nd:
Don went to Wembley to see Nick Van Eede supporting David Essex. Swinn & Debbie & Micky Legg & Rose were also there...

December 11th 1978:
Don found out he had a small fracture in one of his ribs.

21st:
Advision - overdubs on 'My Baby's Got It'.

AUTHOR'S NOTE

This book has combined the years 1977 and 1978 by necessity, because Slade were hardly visible for a huge part of 1977 and it was almost the same in 1978. The years 1979 and 1980 will also be combined in one book.

THANKS

There are a number of people who I would like to thank.

The members of Slade. The Slade book writers. There are some great new books out there. The Slade website people. The 'From Roots To Boots' blog site, which is run by Michael Parker. The few people who actually answered my emails and messages. All the people who ran Slade Fan Club magazines. Nigel, Dee, Davey and Bernie for advice.

I would like to sincerely thank Don Powell for putting his diary entries for these years online. I have quoted just a few of his remarks from a few of the entries, as they are quite interesting.

While doing my research I have found a wealth of Slade reference material on a number of websites and in a number of old magazines. No book would be the same without its reference material. Thank you to the writers for those articles, (for magazines which all seem to be sadly defunct these days), for spreading the gospel of this fine group. While some parts of the content may indeed have been available previously, it has never all been under one roof, so to speak. Most of the content is from the press archives where I seem to spend my daylight hours.

Thanks to gig photographers for use of images as credited. Some are from websites, which I approached for permission for use, but got no reply. They have used in several places, so I have worked on the principle of 'fair usage'. Some local press archives have been wonderfully helpful.

Thanks to the people who offered some self-publishing advice. It's not that easy to get a book out there, so it was very much appreciated.

Thanks for looking at this book, which is totally unofficial. Love to Lisa.

BIBLIOGRAPHY

FEEL THE NOIZE.
Chris Charlesworth. Omnibus.

LOOK WOT I DUN
Lise Lyng Falkenberg. Omnibus.

WHO'S CRAZEE NOW?
Noddy Holder / Lisa Verrico. Ebury.

THE WORLD ACCORDING TO NODDY HOLDER.
Noddy Holder. Constable.

SLADE
George Tremlett. Futura.

THE SLADE PAPERS
Music Sales Ltd.

BRAVO SCRAPBOOK
Rexpert Books.

CUM ON FEEL THE NOIZE
Alan G Parker and Steve Grantley

THE NOIZE Second Edition.
Chris Selby / Ian Edmundson.
Self-publish, Amazon.

SIX YEARS ON THE ROAD
Ian Edmundson.
Self-publish, Amazon.

SLADE IN FLAME
John Pigeon. Panther.

SO HERE IT IS.
Dave Hill. Unbound.

IMAGE RESTORATION

The gig advert images in these books are more often than not from press archives, and they are OLD!! Some are damaged almost irreparably and are nearly impossible to read.

You may not think of it when glancing through these books, but some of these images can take over an hour each to restore to a readable state. Some have actually taken a few attempts. They won't always be one hundred percent perfect, but I have tried my best. I'd like to thank a great Slade fan for invaluable advice. These books wouldn't have appeared without that help.

Also by TONY CHARLES in the SLADE YEAR BY YEAR series.

Watch This Space.....

TONY CHARLES

Tony Charles is the author of this series of Slade books, which aims to cover the period when Slade had a live career.

Married to the ever-patient Lisa and the proud father of two grown-up sons. When they fled to their own homes, to escape the sound of Tony's drums, the empty nest provided some office space and retirement allowed time to browse far-off newspaper archives via the internet and, to his amazement, books started to flow.

Formerly a gas fitter by trade, he has written pieces for a few hobbyist magazines over many years and having retired in 2020, now divides his time between a holiday flat in The Algarve with a really spotty internet connection and the family home in south London.

Tony also has a book on Queen in the works.

Printed in Great Britain
by Amazon